BLUEPRINTS

Maths Key Stage 1 Copymast

CM01603583

Second edition

Wendy and David Clemson

Stanley Thornes (Publishers) Ltd

First published in 1992
Second edition 1995
First published in new binding in 1997 by:
Stanley Thornes (Publishers) Ltd
Ellenborough House
Wellington Street
CHELTENHAM GL50 1YW
England

A catalogue record for this book is available from the British Library.

ISBN 0–7487–3437–6

Typeset by Tech-Set, Gateshead, Tyne & Wear.
Printed and bound in Great Britain by Redwood Books, Trowbridge, Wiltshire

98 99 00 01 02 / 10 9 8 7 6 5 4 3 2

CONTENTS

Contents

INTRODUCTION

In this book there are 113 photocopiable worksheets. C1–C101 are linked specifically to activities in the *Teacher's Resource Book*. C102 is a teacher record sheet. R1–R11 are so called because they are resource copymasters and are intended for use again and again across all sections of the book. Where the photocopy sheets are referred to in the text of the *Teacher's Resource Book* there are some instructions on how to use them. They are referred to by number in the *Teacher's Resource Book* by this symbol: 

When the children have completed these worksheets they can be added to workfiles or used as exemplar material in pupil profiles. You may also wish to use completed worksheets as a resource for your assessments. There is a tick list on copymaster C102, on which you can note the photocopy sheets the children have used.

Name ______________________________

Conservation of 5

Colour and count

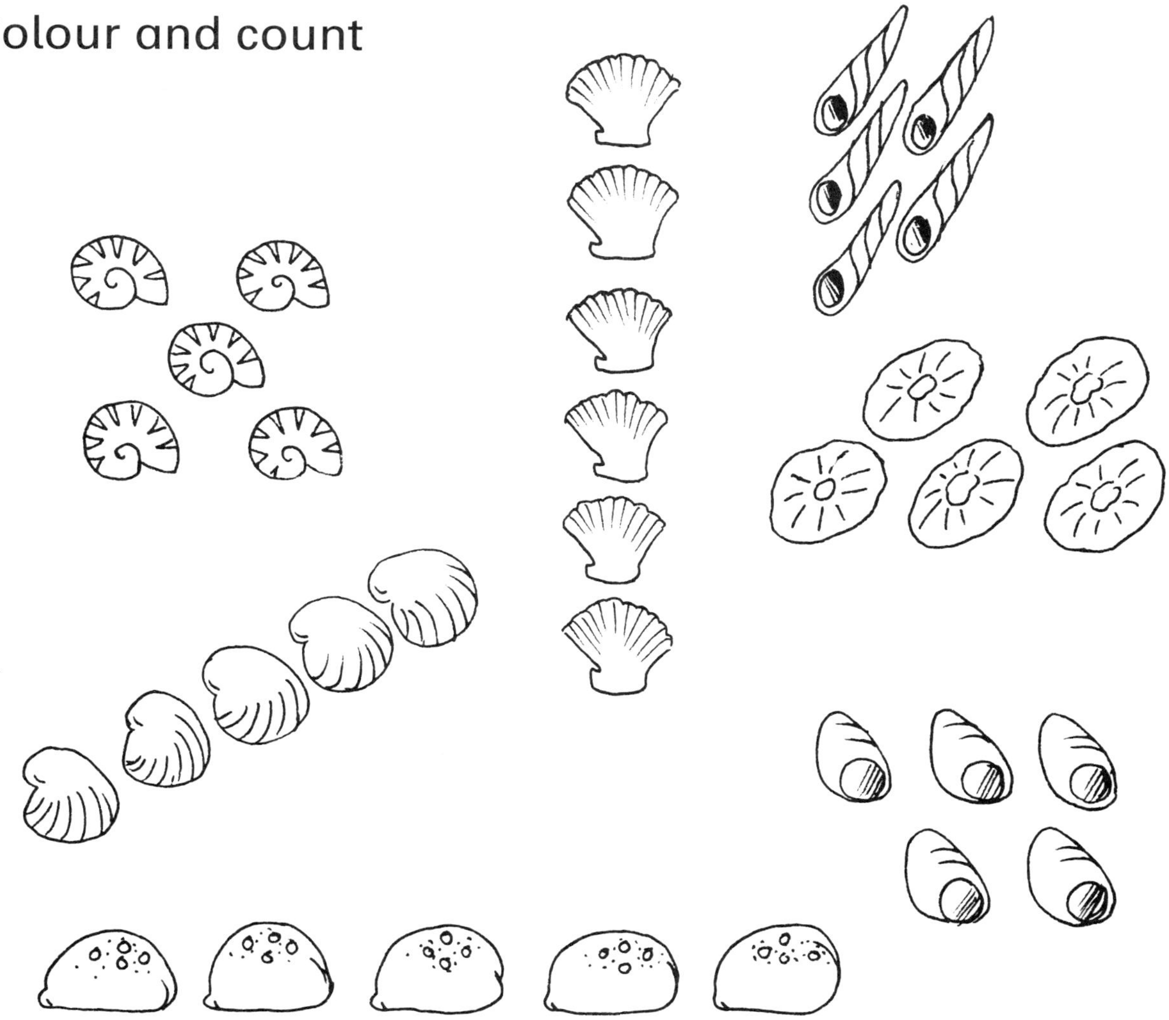

Draw more patterns of 5

Name ______________________________

Conservation of 2, 3, 5

Colour groups of 2 red, 3 blue and 5 green

Name ______________________________

Ladybird race

Name ______________________

Cheese chase

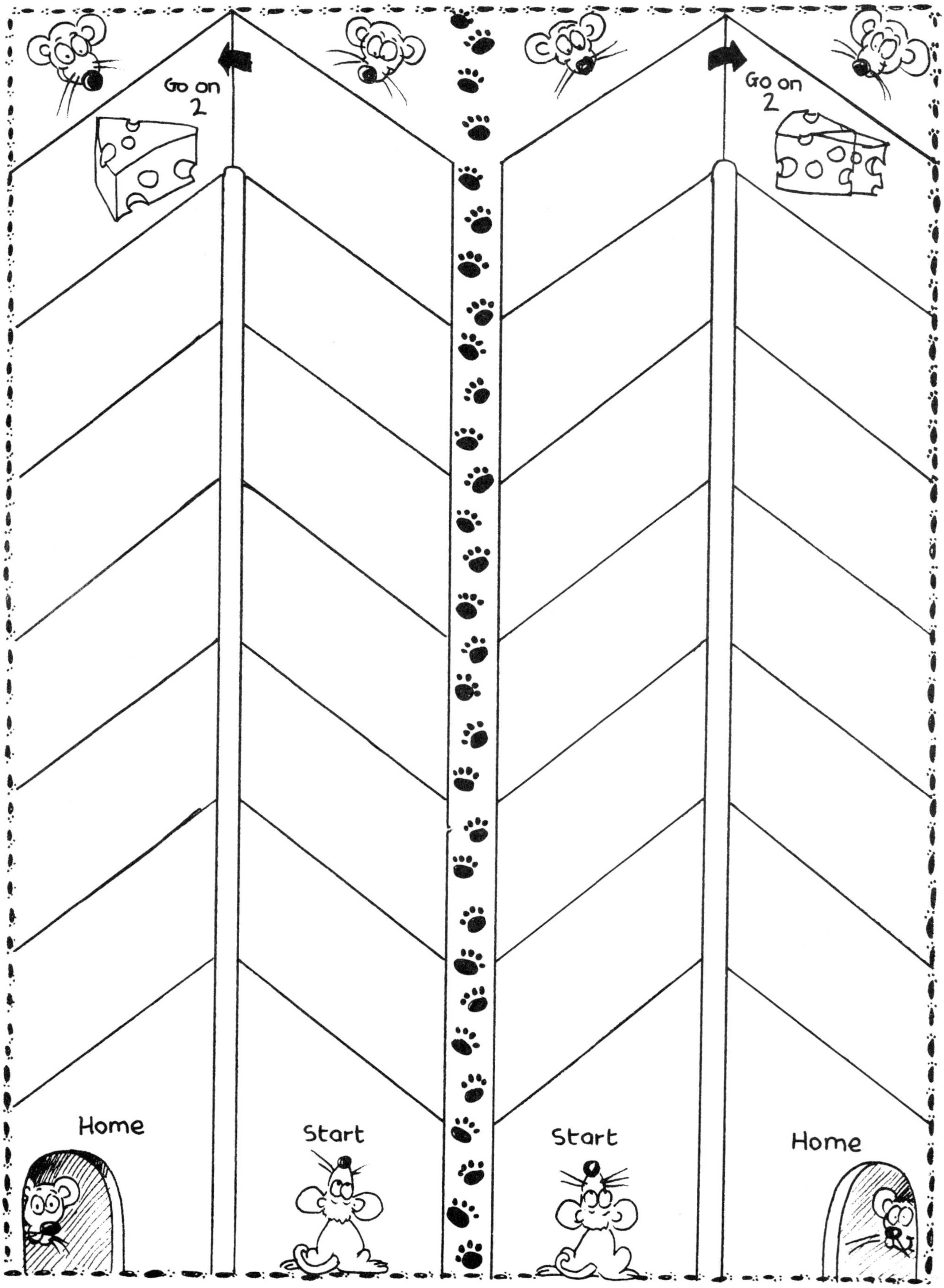

Name ______________________

Home-time!

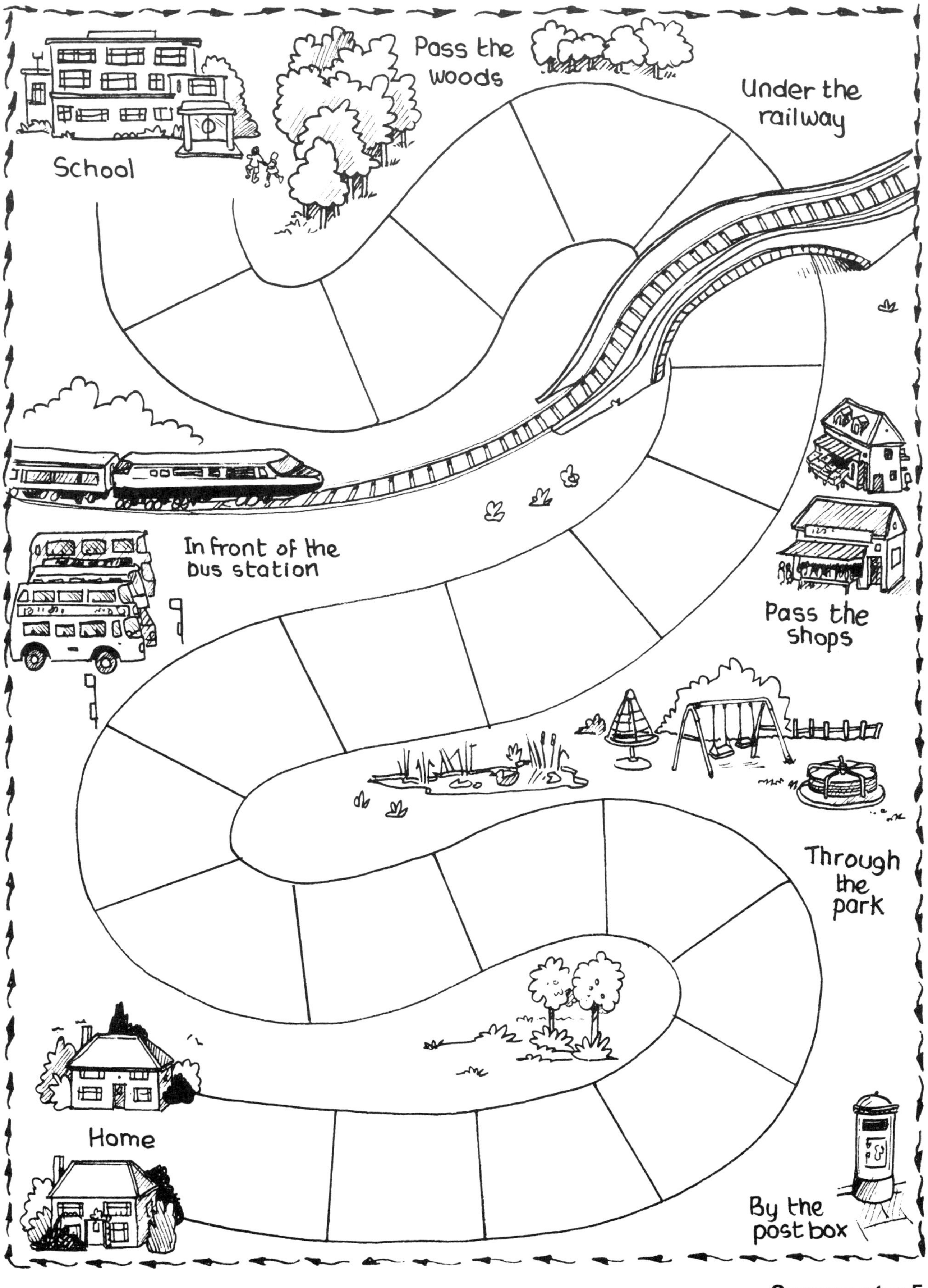

Name ____________________

Aliens

Name ______________________

Odds and evens

Write in – odd or even

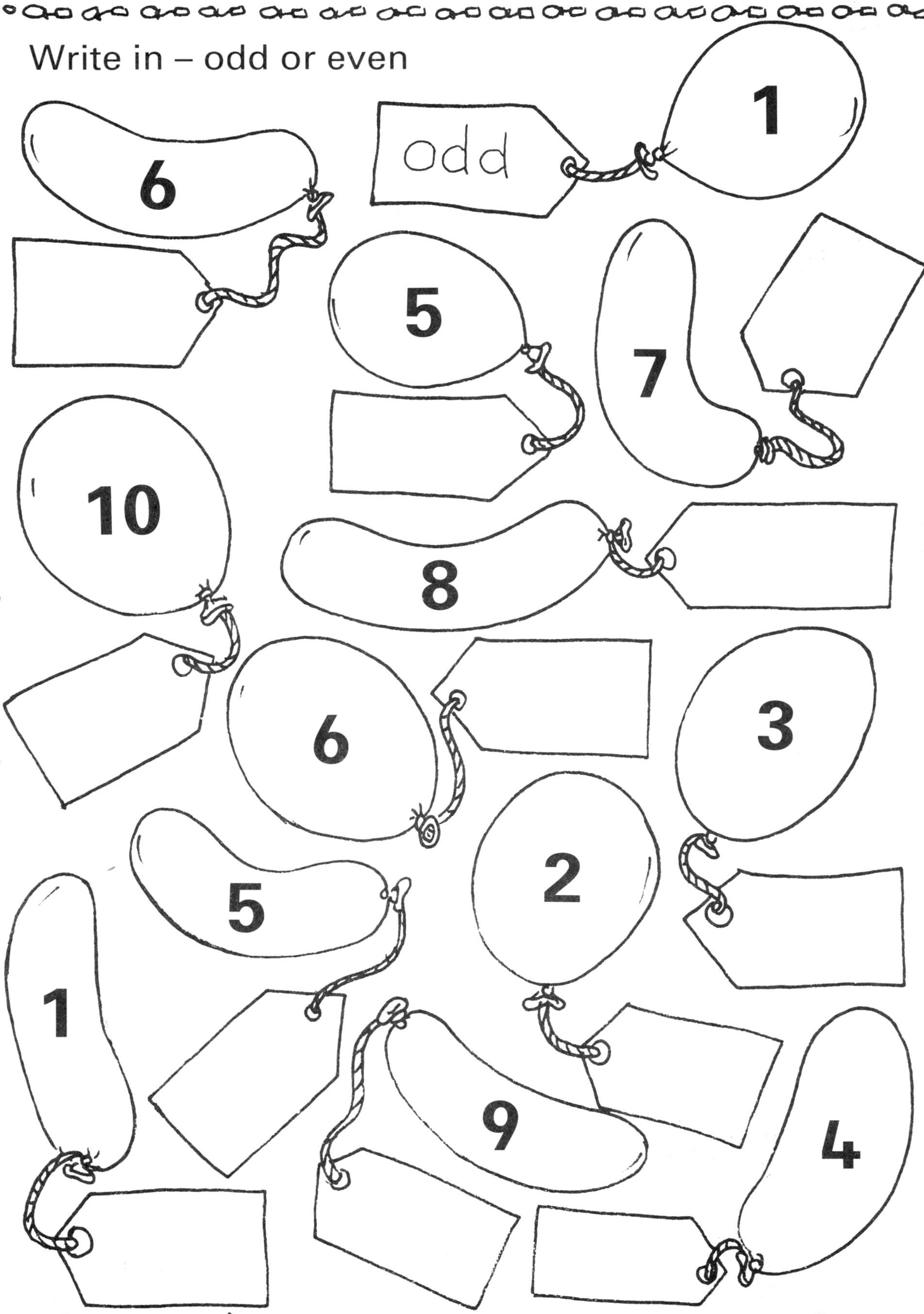

Name ________________________________

Prize winning numbers

Colour the numbers that win a prize

24 6 1 22 3

18 14 4 23 11 8

21 9 12 2

15 7

10 13 19

16 5 17 20 25

Numeral-set match

Match

1

2

3

4

5

6

Name ____________________

Counting and recording counts

How many?

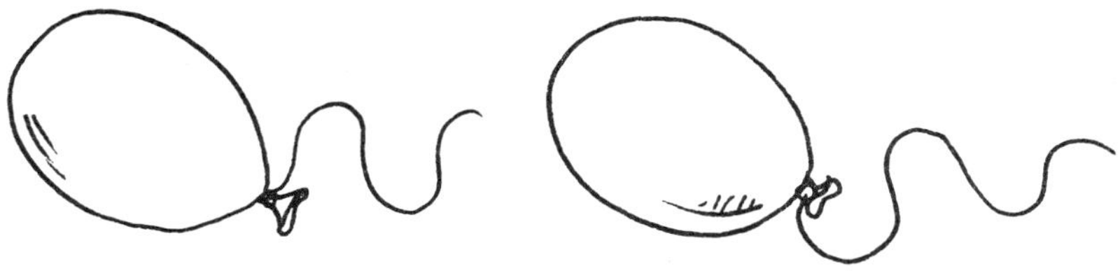

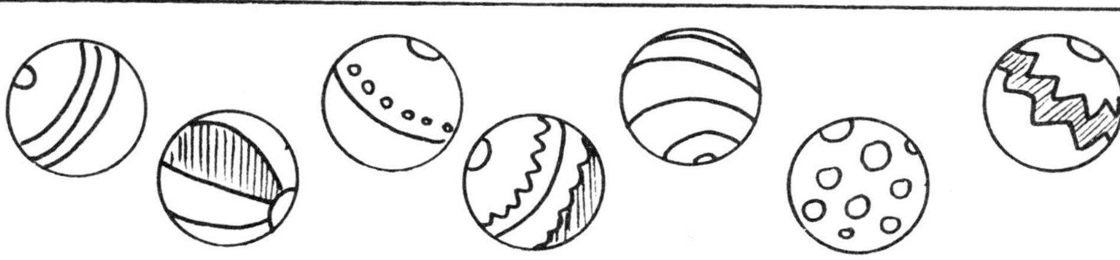

Name ______________________

Counting and recording counts

How many?

eyes		mouths	
ears		faces	
noses		eyebrows	

Name ______________________________

Counting and recording counts

How many?

Name ______________________

Pairs

How many pairs?

☐	pair of eyes
☐	pair of ears
☐	pair of lips
☐	pair of hands
☐	pair of arms
☐	pair of legs
☐	pair of feet
☐	pair of socks
☐	pair of trainers

Name ____________________

Ordinal numbers

Who will win the race?

Write 1st 2nd 3rd by the cars

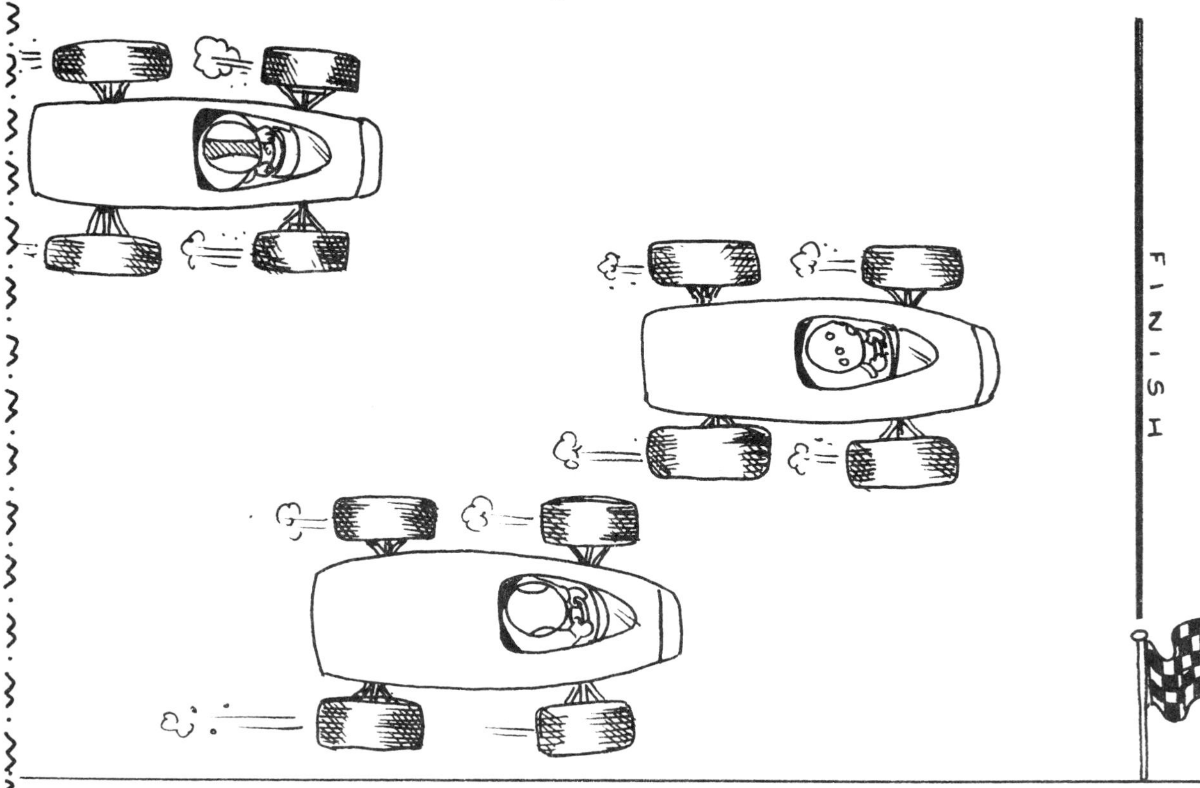

Match

second fourth third first

3rd 1st 4th 2nd

Name ______________________________

Tens and units

Set these out as tens and units

14 27 74 32 46

Look for the pattern

15 25 35 45 55

Which is the biggest number
in these?

19 11 39 91 48

These are easy if you know the pattern

10 20 30 40 50

Name ______________________________

Thousands, hundreds, tens and units

Set these out as hundreds, tens and units

100 105 150 151 501

Try this for size! You need a thousands column

4321

Do these in order of size. Start with the smallest

122 5011 36 95 14

These numbers make a pattern

250 500 750 1000 1250

Name ______________________

Big numbers in words

Write these in numerals

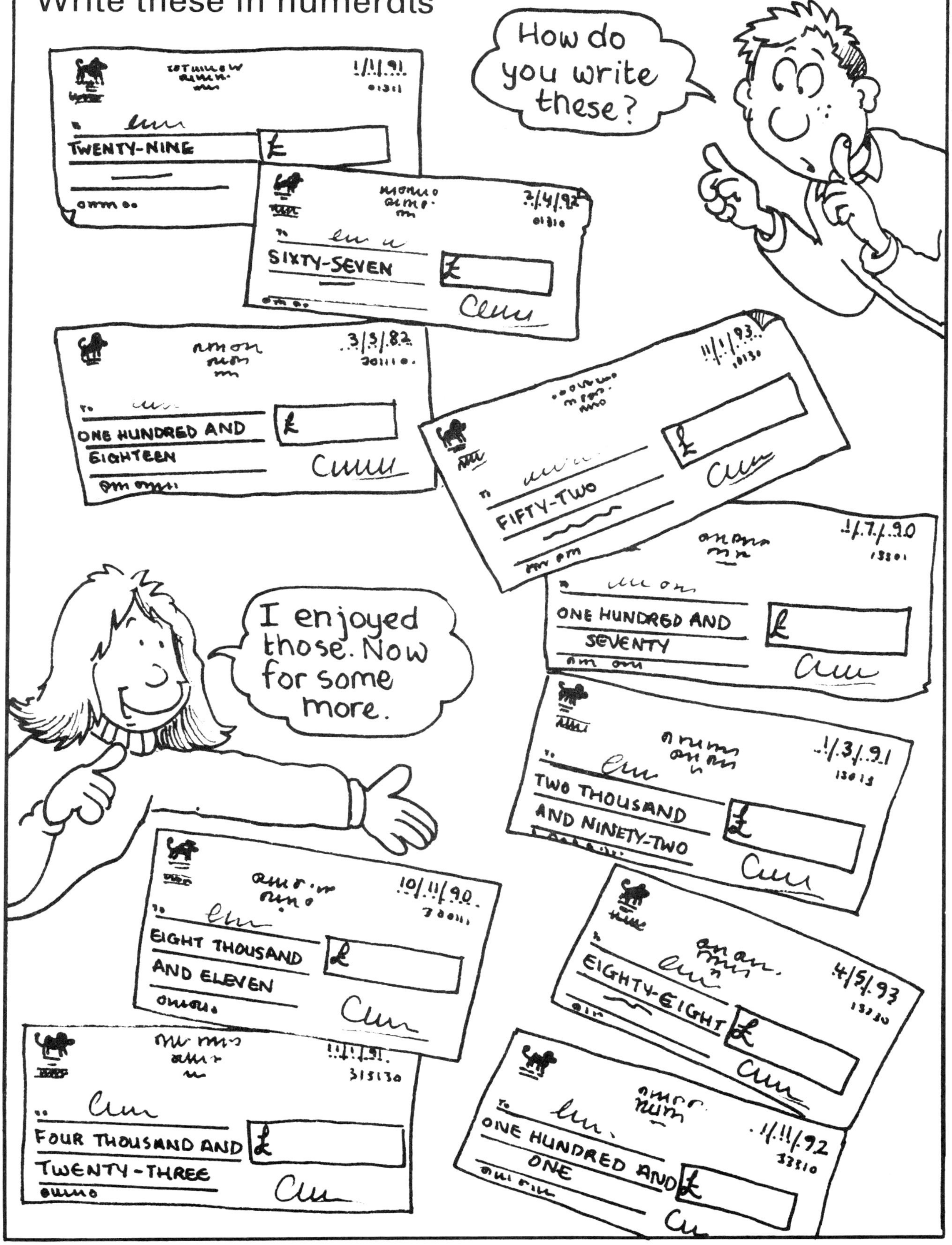

Name ______________________

Halves

Ring a half ($\frac{1}{2}$) of these

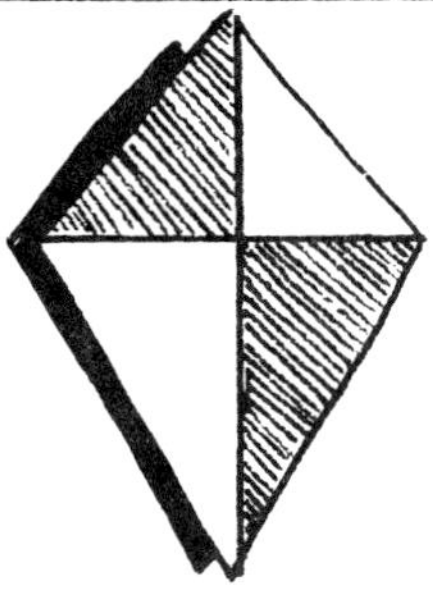 kite	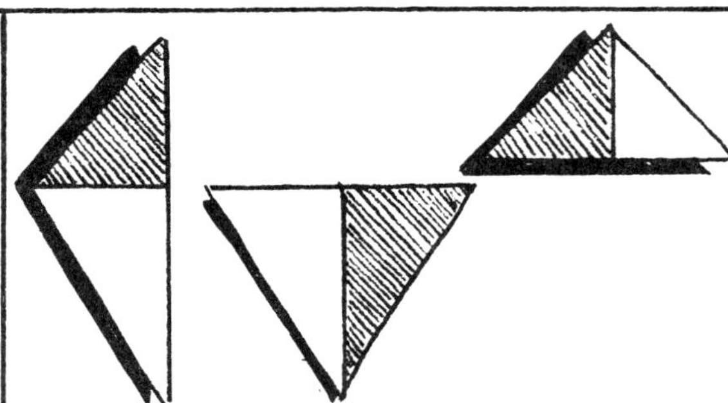
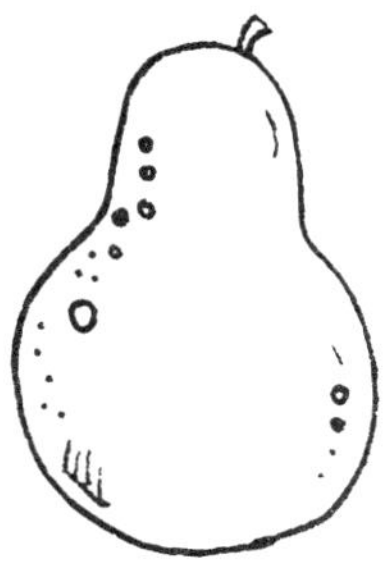 pear	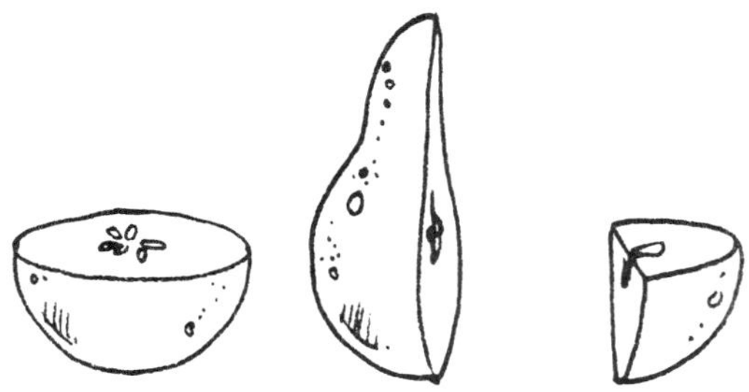
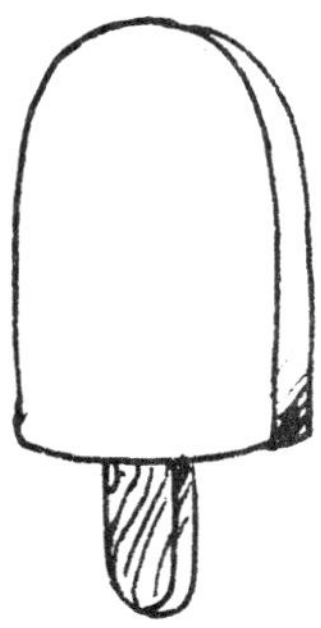 lolly	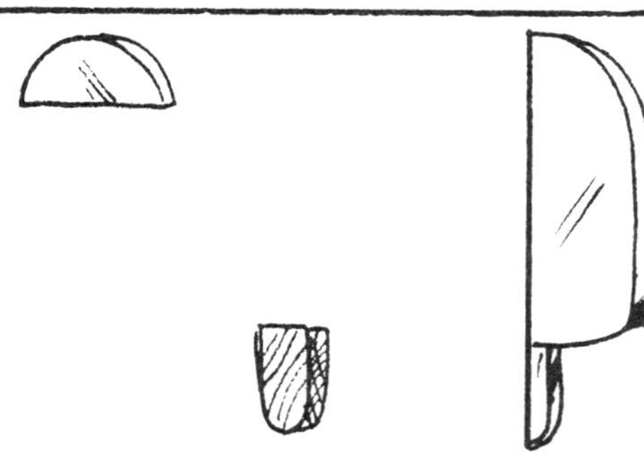
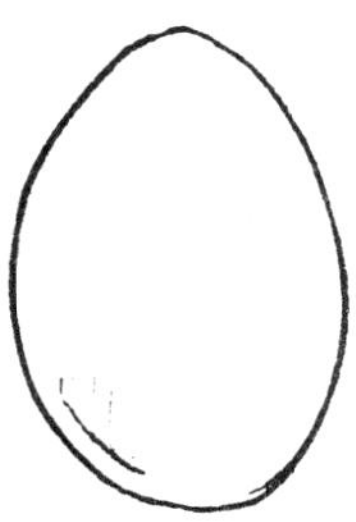 egg	
 piece of paper	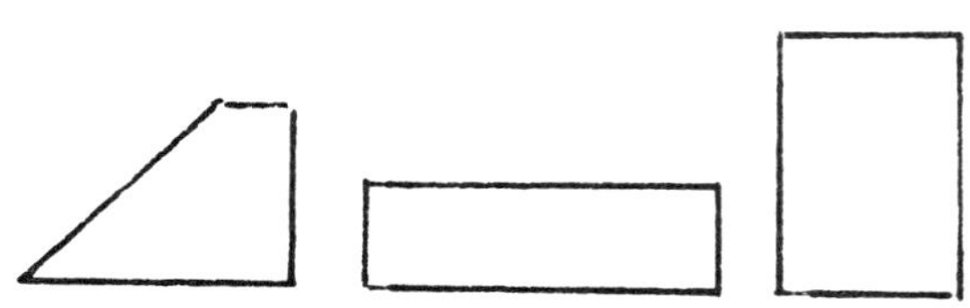

Name ________________________________

Quarters

Ring a quarter ($\frac{1}{4}$) of these

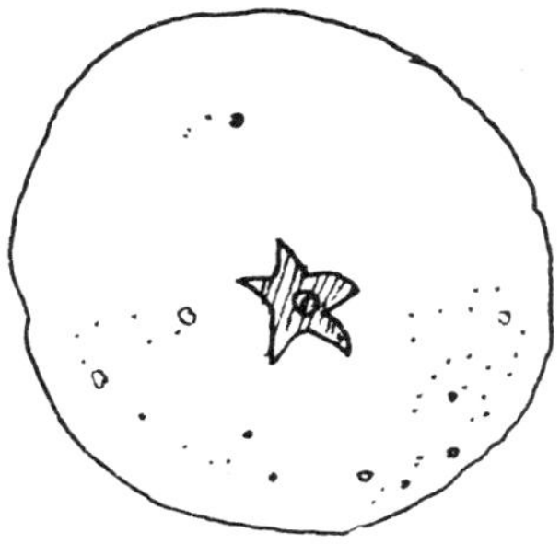

orange

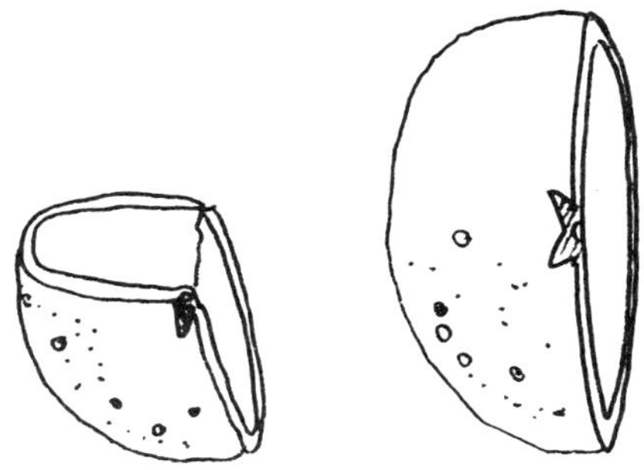

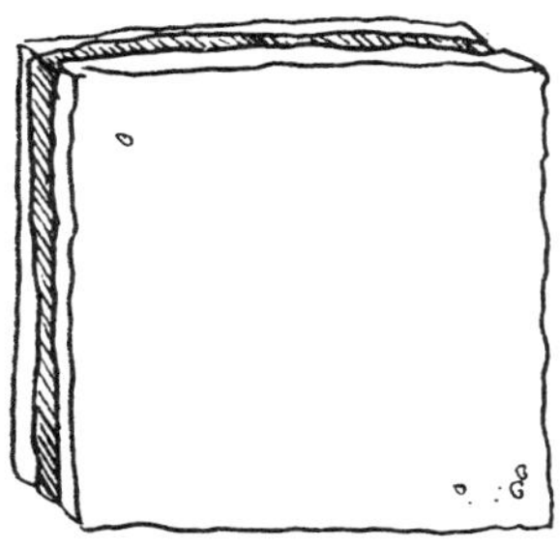

cheese sandwich

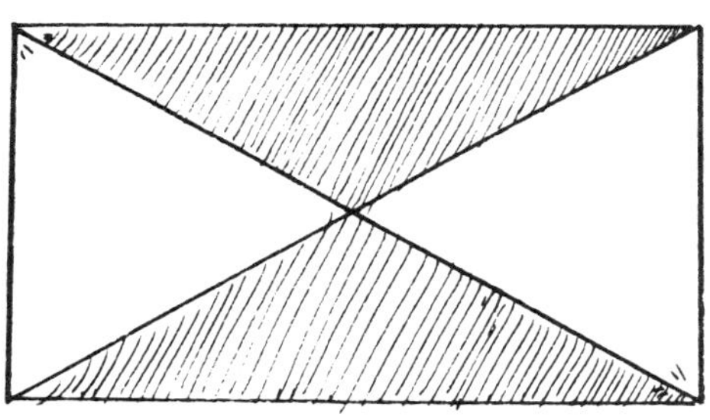

flag

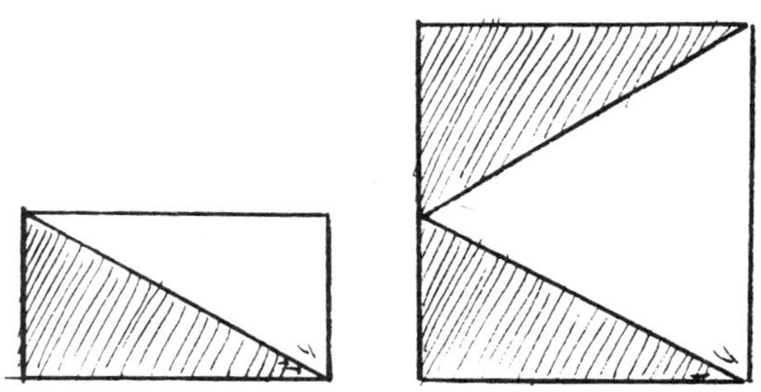

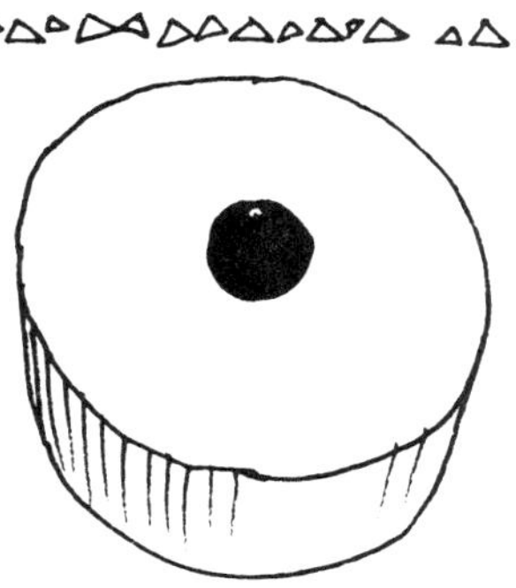

cherry cake

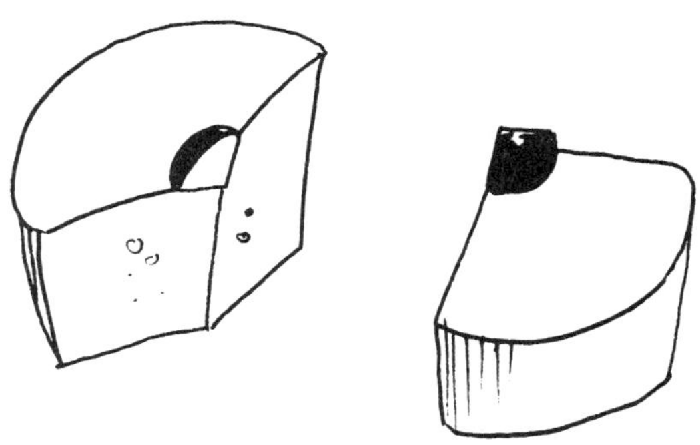

Name ______________________________

Tickets, bills and receipts

A supermarket receipt

	£
Catfood	0.29
Catfood	0.26
Red apples	1.98
Pk. sausages	1.09
Peas	0.79
Fresh chicken	4.12
New potatoes	0.66
Mild cheddar	0.65
Rasp. yogurt	1.03
Balance due	9.87
Cash	10.00
Change	0.13

A bus ticket

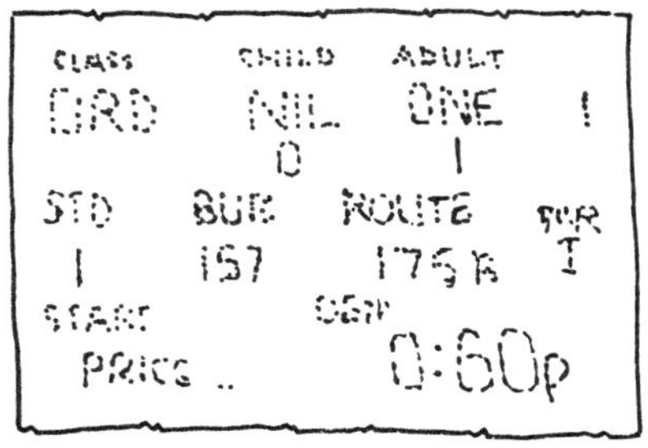

Price tags

A rail ticket

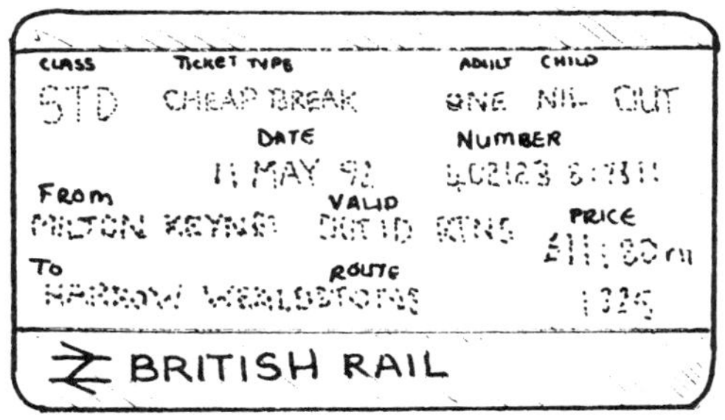

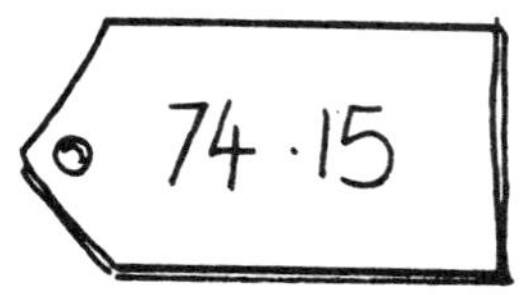

Bar code

95p

Jones the Papers
6, High Street, Newtown
Longshire

DELIVERY ADDRESS
Williams
72, Lower Lane
Newton Longshire

INVOICE NUMBER 1073

	£
Newspapers 14th July to 25th August	25 : 95
Delivery charge	1 : 00
Total Due	26 : 95

Shopping list

Bill

Name ______________________________

Money problems

Robin has 52p. She buys

She has ☐ left.

How much did he spend altogether?

Joan has 50p.

She gives 15p to her sister.

She puts 15p in her piggy bank.

She spends the rest.

How much does she spend?

Cherry cake 14p

Sausage roll 23p

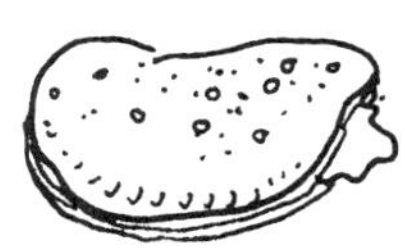

Apple turnover 19p

You have 60p to spend. You may buy more than one of each. Draw what you could have and write how much change you would get.

change ☐	change ☐	change ☐

Name ______________________________

Shopping – track

Name ______________________________

Shopping lists

Toys. Buy these in the toy shop or post office.

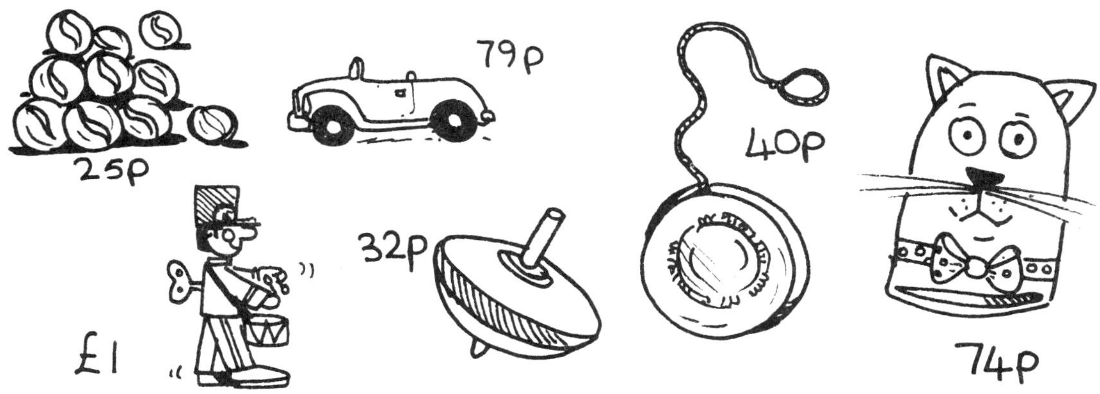

Stationery. Buy these in the toy shop or post office.

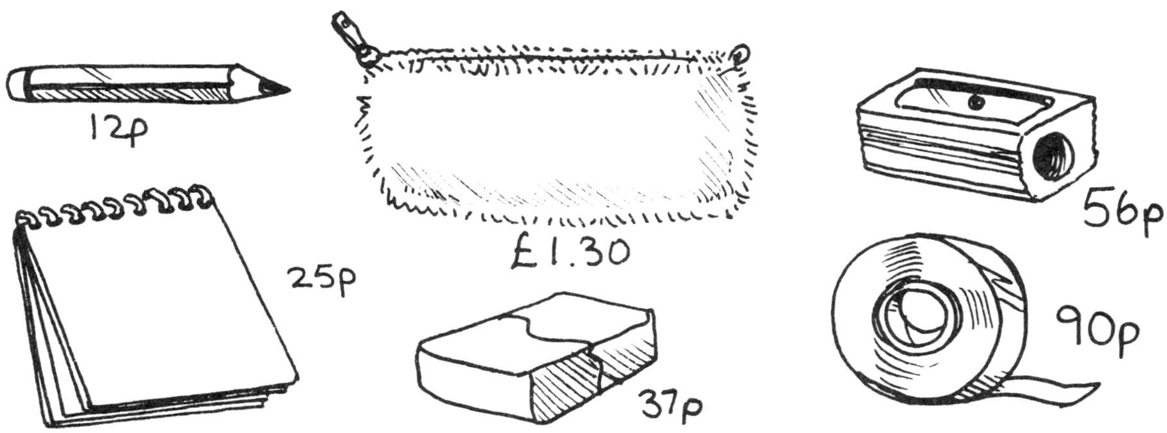

Sweets. Buy these in the sweet shop or post office.

Name ______________________________

Examples with some negative numbers

20 + 0 = ☐   9 + 4 = ☐   11 − 15 = ☐

17 − 7 = ☐   5 − 8 = ☐

8 − 9 = ☐

4 − 5 = ☐   3 + 6 = ☐

10 − 5 = ☐   6 − 7 = ☐

12 + 6 = ☐

2 + 11 = ☐   ☐ = 9 + 9

13 + 5 = ☐   ☐ = 9 − 11

7 − 10 = ☐   ☐ = 8 − 2

Name ______________________________

Patterns around you

Can you find these patterns in things around you?

Where? Draw or write.

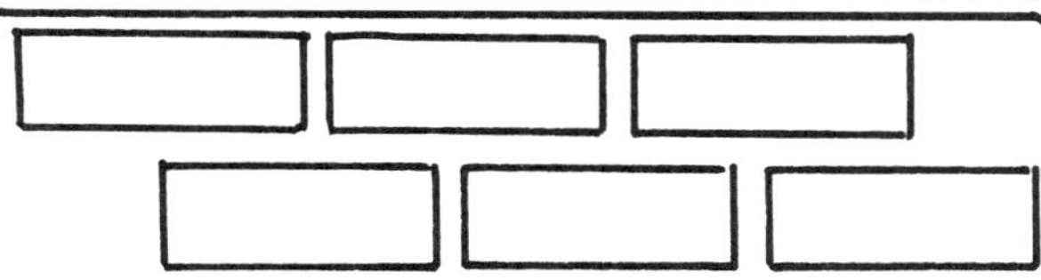

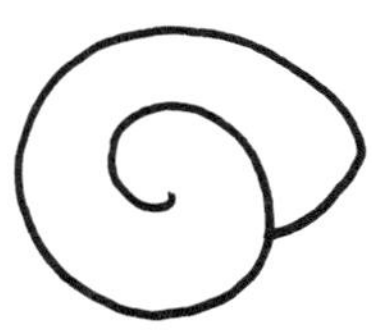

121212

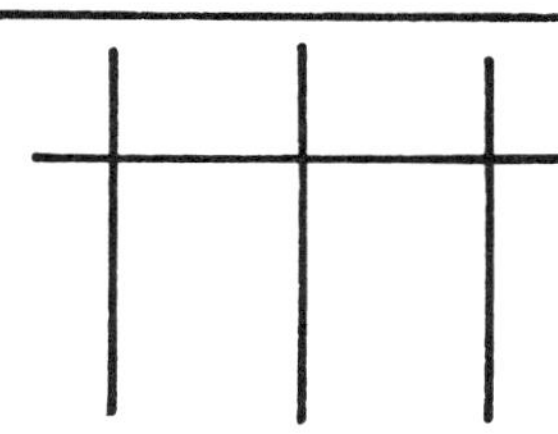

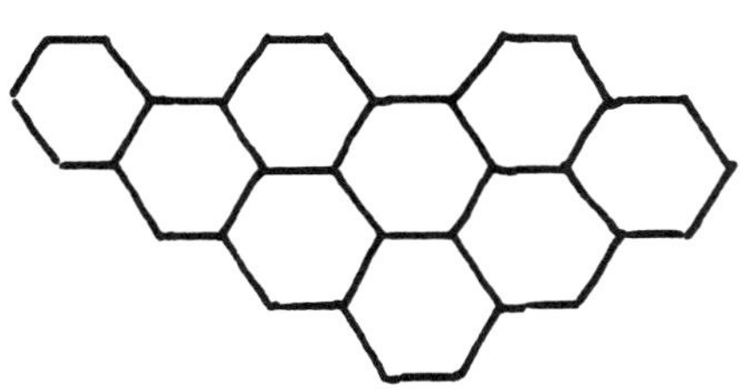

Name ______________________

Number patterns

Continue the patterns. Then play and check.

1 2 3 1 2 3 ______________________

4 6 4 6 4 6 ______________________

3 5 1 3 5 1 ______________________

7 2 7 2 7 2 ______________________

5 1 5 1 ______________________

6 2 6 2 ______________________

2 3 2 3 ______________________

7 3 7 3 1 7 3 7 3 1 ______________________

5 4 3 8 5 4 3 8 ______________________

1 2 1 3 1 2 1 3 ______________________

1 2 3 4 5 1 2 3 4 5 ______________________

Name ______________________________

Number bonds

Make 5 0 + 5 1 + 2 + 3 + 4 + 5 + Make 10 0 + 10 1 + 2 + 3 + 4 + 5 + 6 + 7 + 8 + 9 + 10 +	Make 2 0 + 2 1 + 2 + Make 5 10 − 9 − 8 − 7 − 6 − 5 − Make 5 − 0 − 1 − 2 − 3 − 4 − 5	Make 3 0 + 3 1 + 2 + 3 + Make 7 10 − 9 − 8 − 7 − Make 7 − 0 − 1 − 2 − 3	Make 4 0 + 4 1 + 2 + 3 + 4 + Make 6 10 − 9 − 8 − 7 − 6 − Make 6 − 0 − 1 − 2 − 3 − 4

Name ____________________

Number arrays

Continue the patterns

0, 5, 10, __, __, __, __, __, __, __, __

0, 2, 4, __, __, __, __, __, __, __, __

0, 3, 6, __, __, __, __, __, __, __, __

0, 10, 20, __, __, __, __, __, __, __, __

2 + 10 = 12

12 + 10 =

22 + 10 =

32 + 10 =

90 − 10 = 80

80 − 10 =

70 − 10 =

60 − 10 =

What is missing?

30, 35, 40, __, __, 55, __, __, __

24, 26, __, __, __, 34, 36, __, __

42, 45, 48, __, __, __, __

100, 90, __, __, __, __, __, __

27, 24, 21, __, __, __, __, __

20, 18, 16, __, __, __, __, __, __

Leap frog

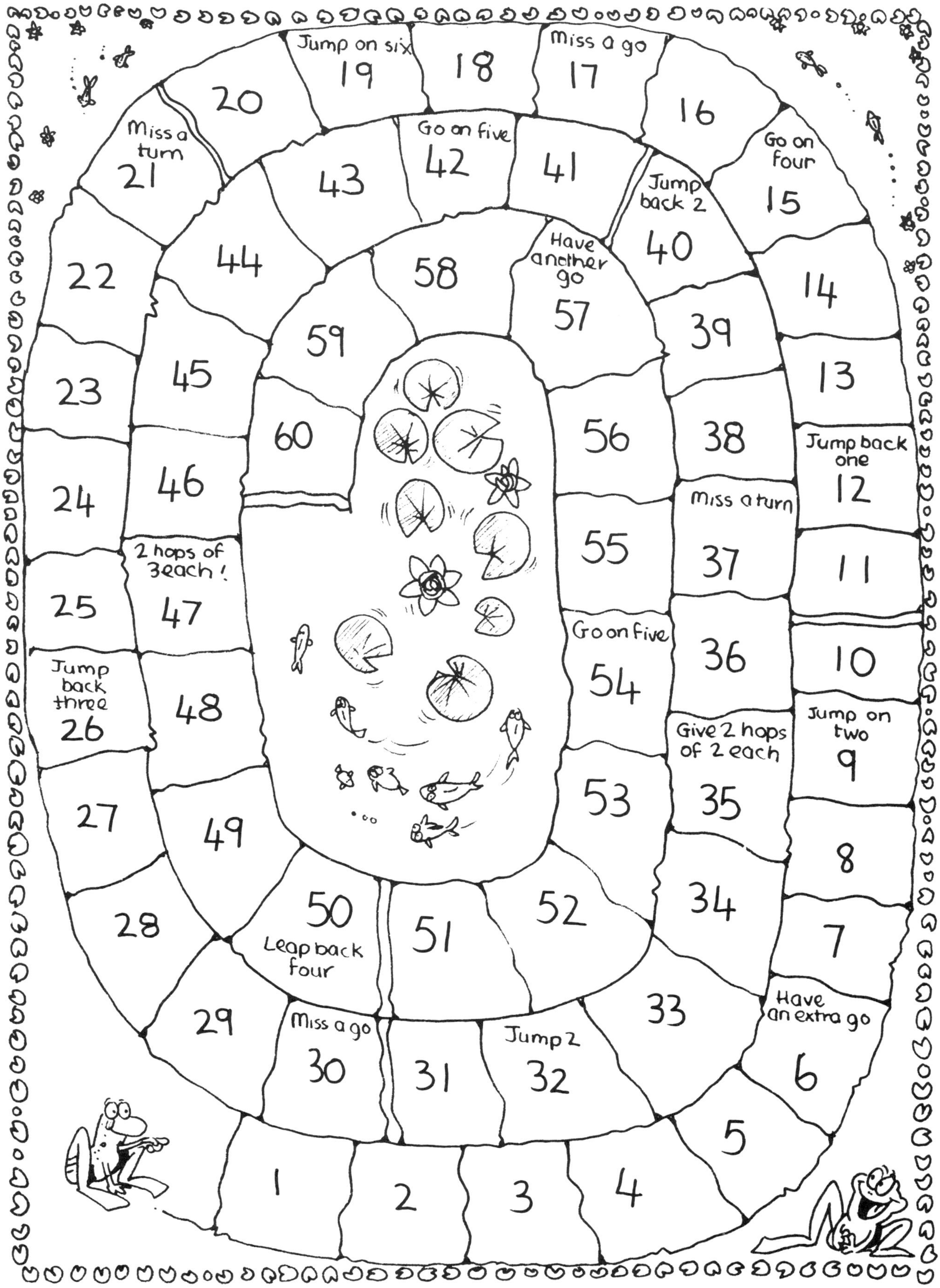
1
2
3
4
5
Have an extra go 6
7
8
Jump on two 9
10
11
Jump back one 12
13
14
Go on four 15
16
Miss a go 17
18
Jump on six 19
20
Miss a turn 21
22
23
24
25
Jump back three 26
27
28
29
Miss a go 30
31
Jump 2 32
33
34
Give 2 hops of 2 each 35
36
Miss a turn 37
38
39
Jump back 2 40
41
Go on five 42
43
44
45
46
2 hops of 3 each! 47
48
49
50 Leap back four
51
52
53
Go on five 54
55
56
Have another go 57
58
59
60

Name ________________________

Planes and parachutes

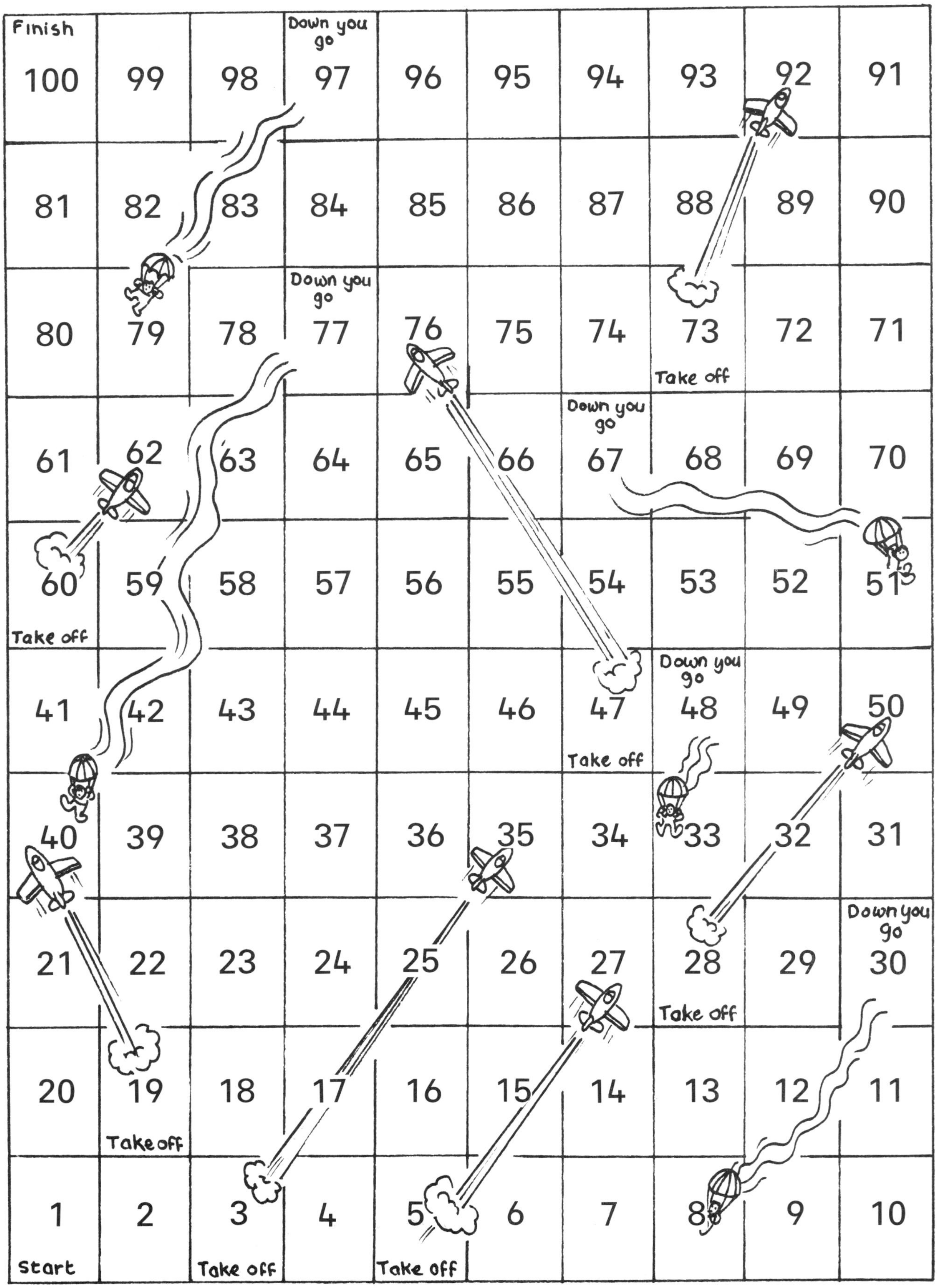

Name ______________________

Take away strips

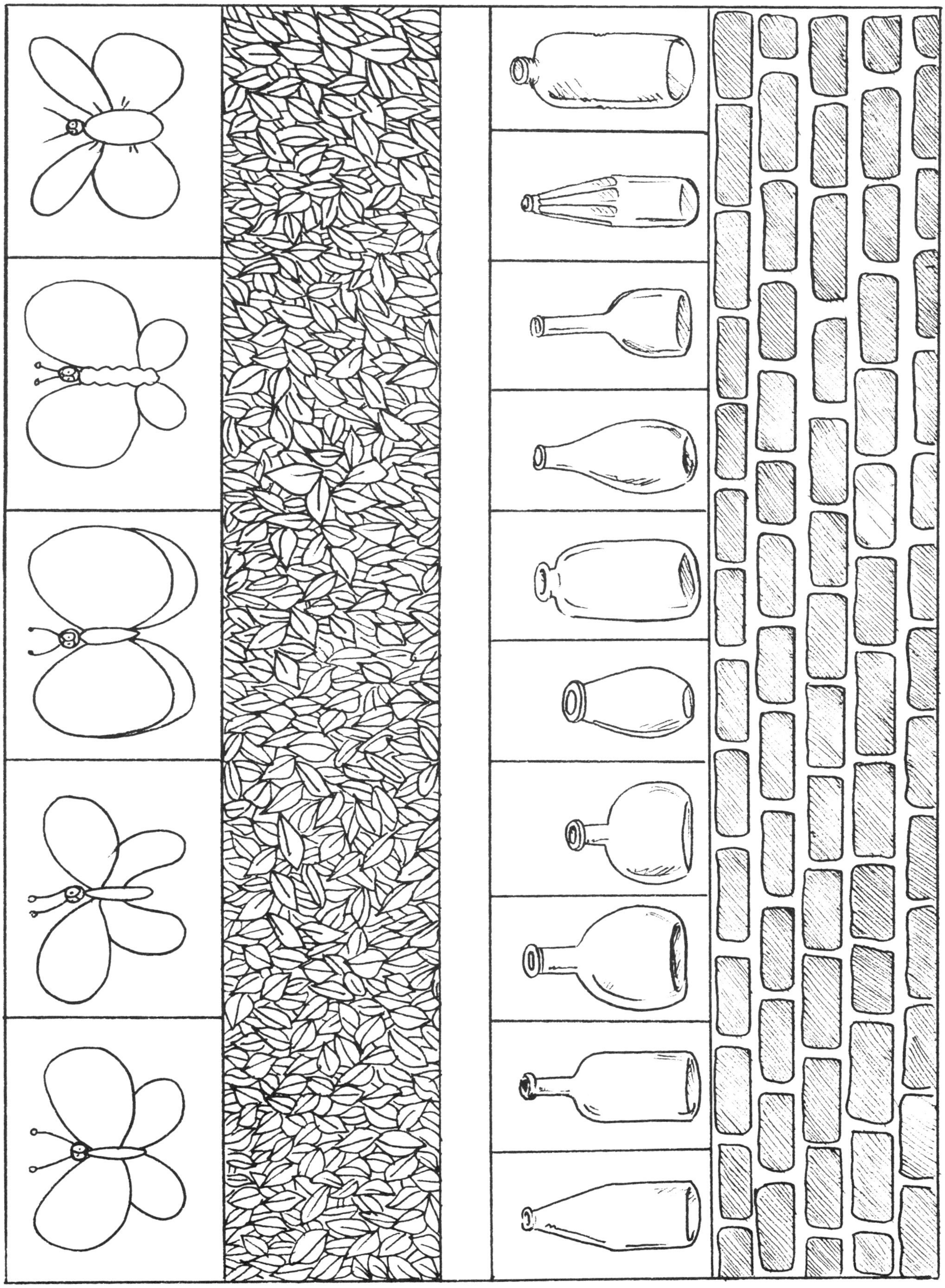

Name ______________________

Make five

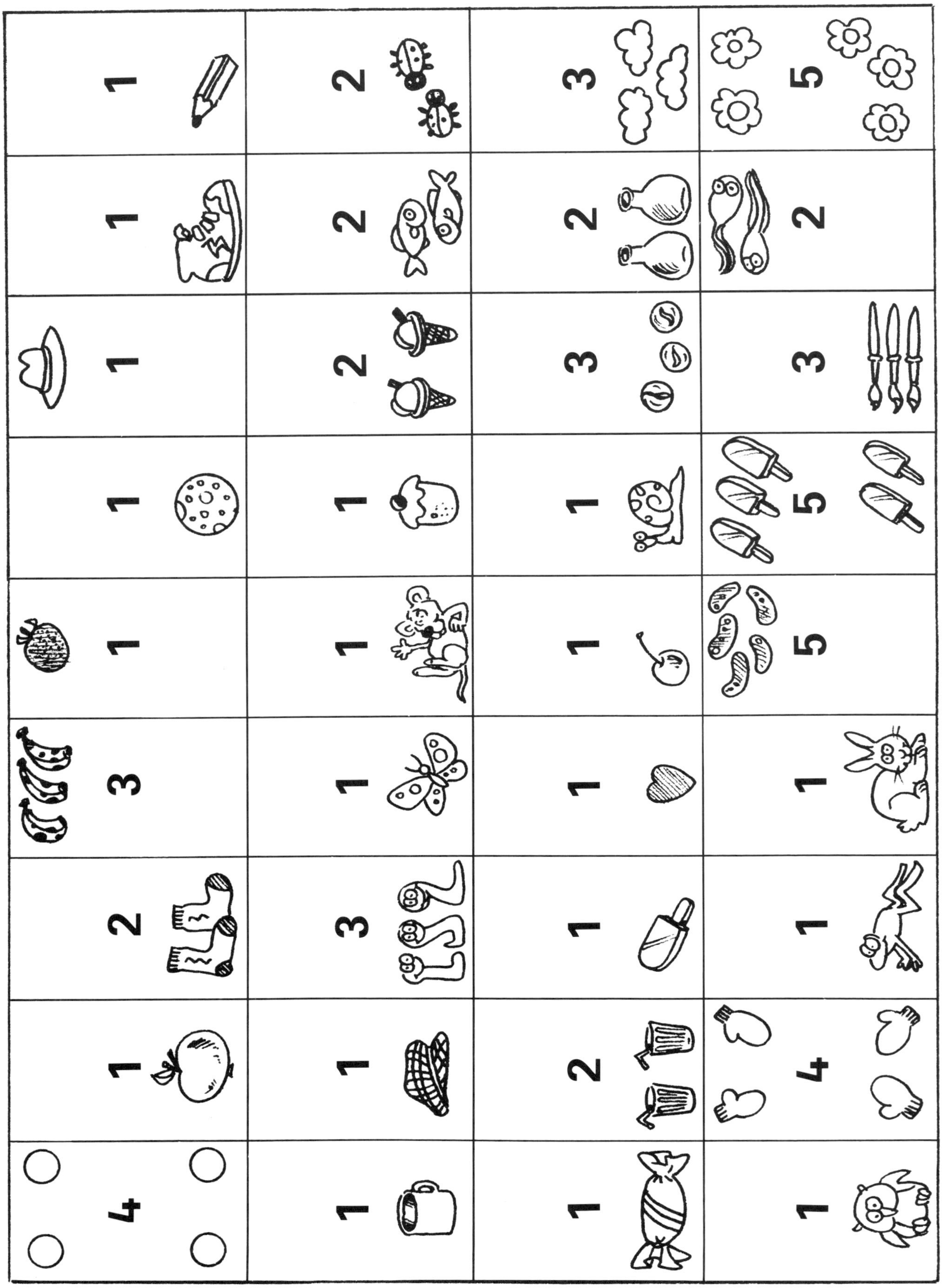

Name ______________________

Make ten

9	1	8	2
7	3	6	4
5	5	4	6
5	5	3	7
2	8	9	1
2	3	5	4
1	5	6	3
1	8	1	1
7	2	1	9

Name ______________________________

Subtraction bonds to 20

20 – 10	20 – 5	20 – 0	20 – 20

Join up like this

20 10 0 15

20 – 8	20 – 6	20 – 4	20 – 2

18 14 16 12

20 – 18	20 – 16	20 – 14	20 – 12

4 2 6 8

20 – 19	20 – 17	20 – 15	20 – 13

5 1 3 7

20 – 11	20 – 9	20 – 7	20 – 3

11 9 17 13

Bingo

Base cards

17 − 11	10 − 5	4 + 2
7 + 8	13 − 3	10 + 10

5 − 5	18 − 7	9 + 5
7 − 3	14 + 2	12 + 8

19 − 7	15 − 5	8 + 2
5 − 0	16 + 3	8 + 9

20 − 10	9 − 6	17 − 9
4 + 12	8 − 5	10 − 10

Numerals

6	5	6	0	11	14
15	10	20	4	16	20
12	10	10	10	3	8
5	19	17	16	3	0

Name ______________________________

Missing numbers

0, 2, _____, 6, 8, _____, _____, 14, 16, _____, 20

0, 3, 6, _____, _____, 15, 18, 21, _____, _____, _____

0, 4, _____, 12, _____, 20, _____, 28, _____, 36, _____

0, 5, 10, _____, _____, _____, 30, 35, 40, _____, _____

0, 6, _____, 18, _____, 30, _____, 42, 48, 54, 60

0, 7, 14, _____, _____, 35, _____, _____, 56, _____, 70

0, 8, _____, _____, 32, 40, _____, _____, 64, 72, _____

0, 9, _____, 27, 36, _____, _____, 63, 72, _____, 90

0, 10, _____, _____, _____, 50, 60, 70, _____, _____, _____

What's next in the pattern?

9, 12, 15, _____ 35, 42, _____ 60, 70, _____

10, 12, _____ 20, 25, _____ 8, 16, _____

Name ______________________________

Zap!

Name ______________________________

Multiply cards for Zap

1 × 2	2 × 2	3 × 2	4 × 2
5 × 2	6 × 2	7 × 2	8 × 2
9 × 2	10 × 2	1 × 3	3 × 3
4 × 3	5 × 3	6 × 3	7 × 3
8 × 3	9 × 3	10 × 3	1 × 5
4 × 5	5 × 5	6 × 5	7 × 5
8 × 5	9 × 5	10 × 5	1 × 10
4 × 10	6 × 10	7 × 10	8 × 10
9 × 10	10 × 10		

Name ______________________________

Multiplication ladders

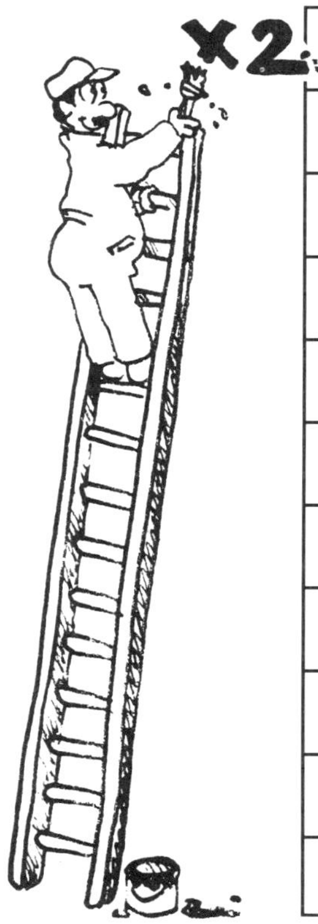

0 × 2 = 0
1 × 2 =
2 × 2 =
3 × 2 =
4 × 2 =
5 × 2 =
6 × 2 =
7 × 2 =
8 × 2 =
9 × 2 =
10 × 2 =

0 × 3 = 0
1 × 3 =
2 × 3 =
3 × 3 =
4 × 3 =
5 × 3 =
6 × 3 =
7 × 3 =
8 × 3 =
9 × 3 =
10 × 3 =

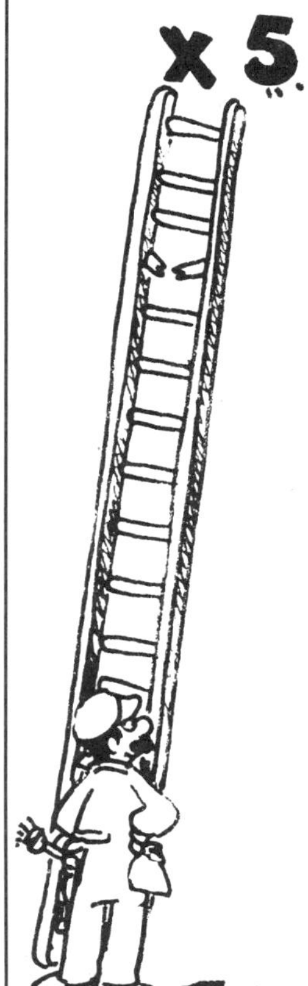

0 × 5 = 0
1 × 5 =
2 × 5 =
3 × 5 =
4 × 5 =
5 × 5 =
6 × 5 =
7 × 5 =
8 × 5 =
9 × 5 =
10 × 5 =

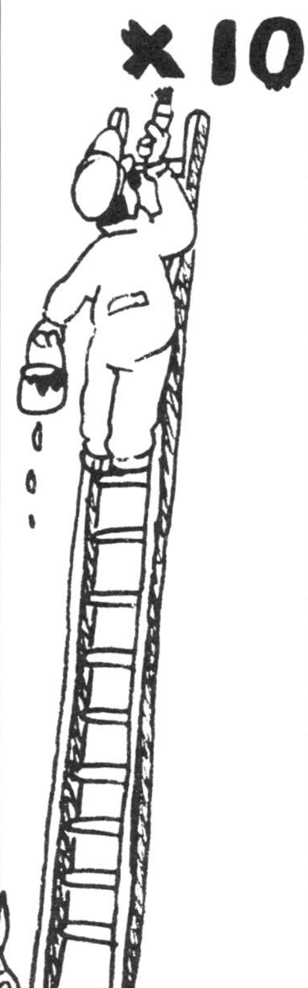

0 × 10 = 0
1 × 10 =
2 × 10 =
3 × 10 =
4 × 10 =
5 × 10 =
6 × 10 =
7 × 10 =
8 × 10 =
9 × 10 =
10 × 10 =

Name ______________________________

Picture sharing

Ann Roberta Liam

Lollipops. How many each? ☐

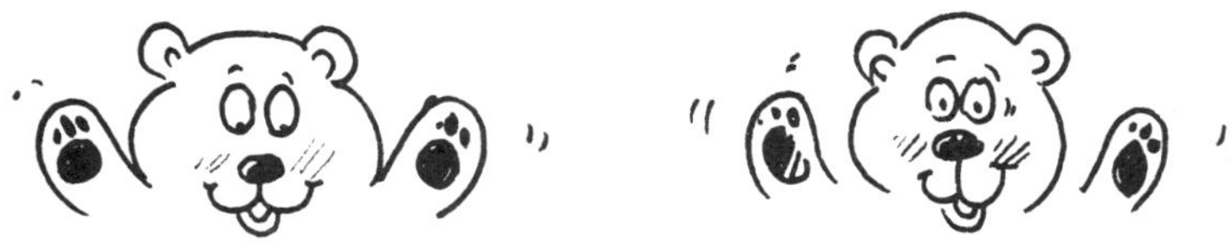

Ed Fred

Honey pots. How many each? ☐

Worms. How many each? ☐

Cherries. How many each? ☐

Name ______________________________

Division puzzles

20 bones

- 2 dogs ☐ each
- 4 dogs ☐ each
- 5 dogs ☐ each
- 10 dogs ☐ each

21p

- 3 boys ☐ p each
- 7 girls ☐ p each

30 people

- 2 minibuses ☐ in each
- 3 minibuses ☐ in each
- 5 minibuses ☐ in each
- 6 minibuses ☐ in each
- 10 minibuses ☐ in each

Name ______________________

Divide cards for Zap

2 ÷ 4	4 ÷ 2	6 ÷ 2	8 ÷ 2
10 ÷ 2	12 ÷ 2	14 ÷ 2	16 ÷ 2
18 ÷ 2	20 ÷ 2	3 ÷ 3	6 ÷ 3
9 ÷ 3	12 ÷ 3	15 ÷ 3	18 ÷ 3
21 ÷ 3	24 ÷ 3	27 ÷ 3	30 ÷ 3
5 ÷ 5	10 ÷ 5	15 ÷ 5	20 ÷ 5
25 ÷ 5	30 ÷ 5	35 ÷ 5	40 ÷ 5
45 ÷ 5	50 ÷ 5	10 ÷ 10	50 ÷ 10
100 ÷ 10			

Name ______________________________

Calculator checks

Check these using a calculator

Give a tick for correct answers
Cross out wrong answers
Write in the correct answer

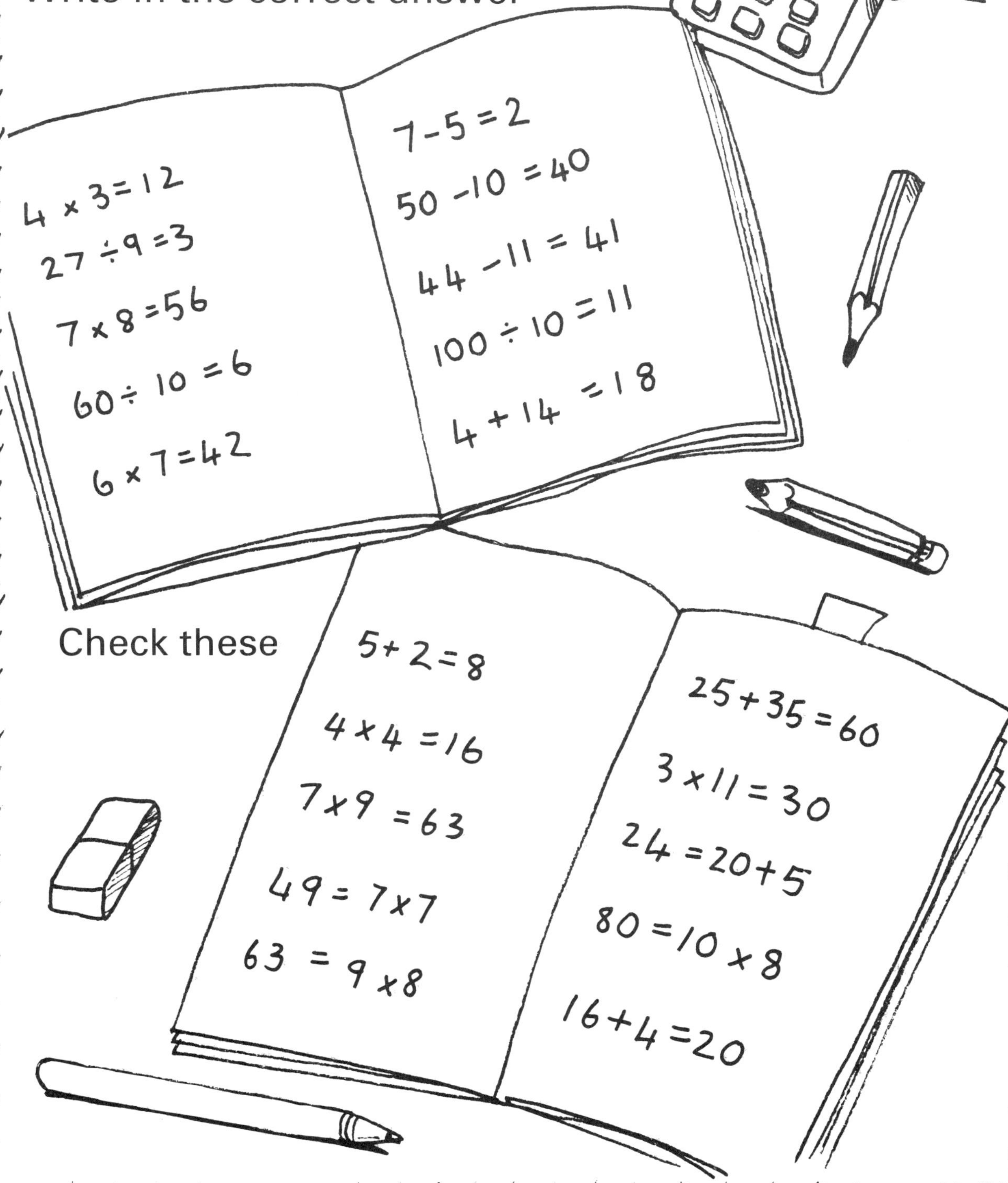

Name ______________________________

Missing number mysteries

Find the missing numbers

$5 + \quad = 8$

$7 + \quad = 10$

$4 + \quad = 6$

$\quad + 4 = 8$

$\quad + 1 = 3$

$3 - \quad = 2$

$7 - \quad = 6$

$2 - \quad = 1$

$\quad - 5 = 5$

$\quad - 7 = 1$

$5 + \quad = 9$

$2 + \quad = 4$

$3 + \quad = 9$

$\quad + 5 = 6$

$\quad + 2 = 7$

$8 - \quad = 5$

$9 - \quad = 7$

$\quad - 4 = 3$

$\quad - 2 = 8$

$\quad - 1 = 3$

Name ____________________

An add 3 robot

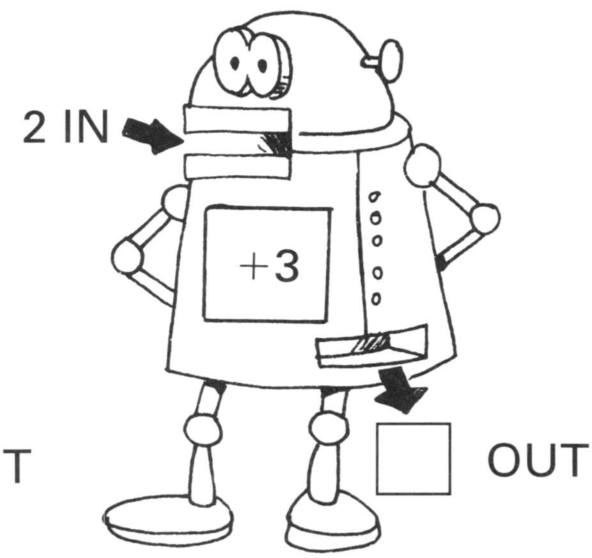

Name ________________________________

A take away 2 machine

3 IN

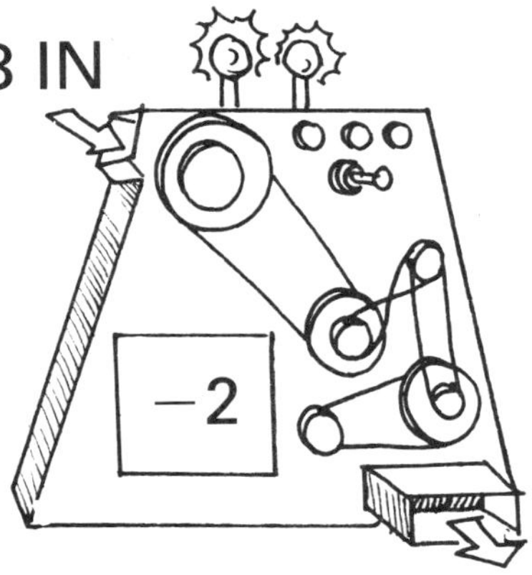

☐ OUT

9 IN

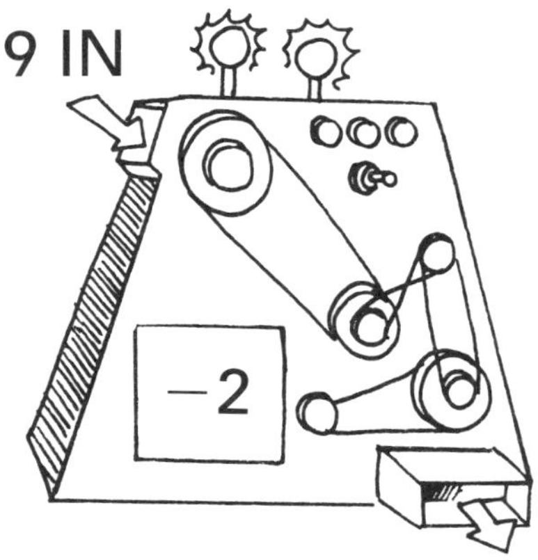

☐ OUT

8 IN

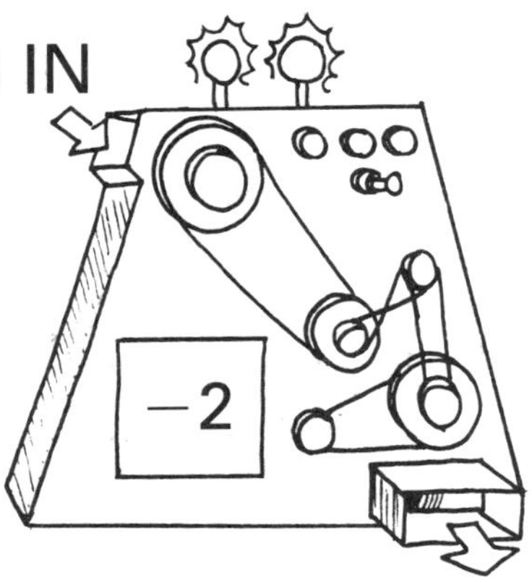

☐ OUT

6 IN

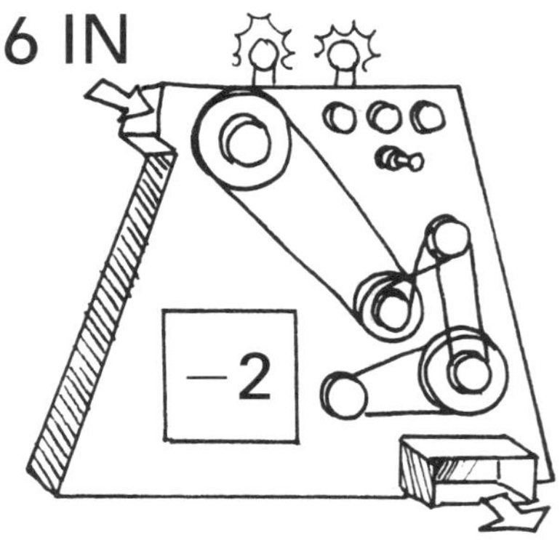

☐ OUT

7 IN

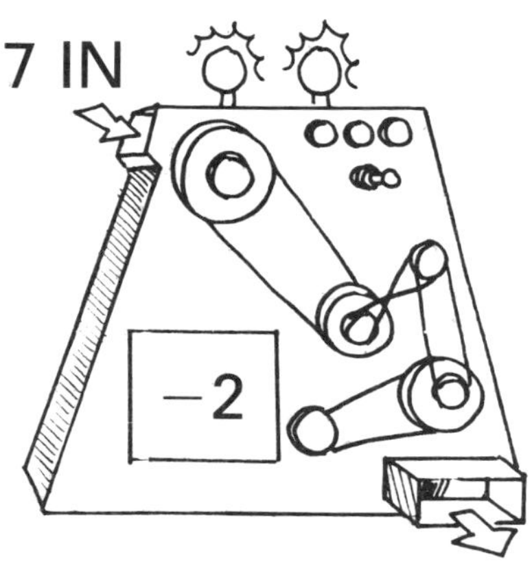

☐ OUT

4 IN

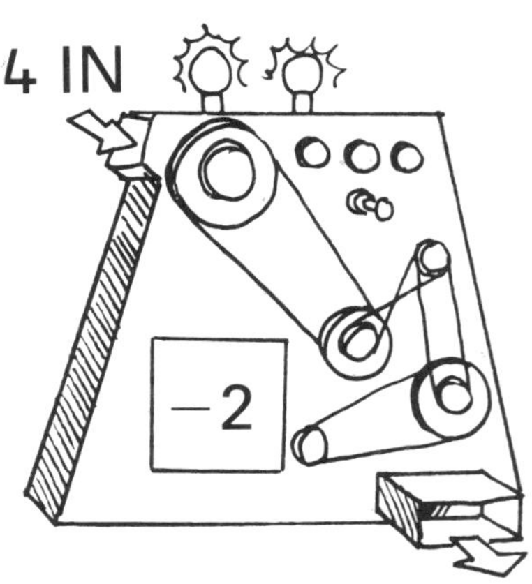

☐ OUT

Name ______________________________

Computation trail

Name ______________________________

Add and subtract

10 − 3 →

7 − 1 →

5 − 2 →

8 − 4 →

9 − 5 →

2 − 1 →

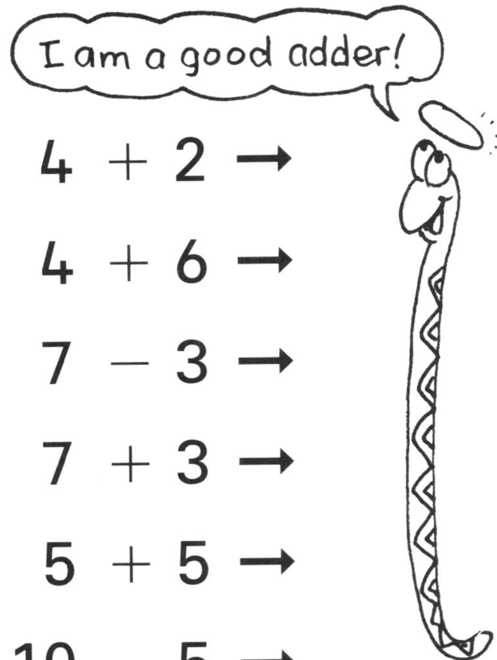

4 + 2 →

4 + 6 →

7 − 3 →

7 + 3 →

5 + 5 →

10 − 5 →

9 − 6 →

What is missing?

7 − □ → 4

4 + □ → 8

6 + □ → 10

□ + 2 → 5

□ + 5 → 7

□ + 3 → 9

Put in the sign + or −?

5   5 → 10

6   2 → 4

7   2 → 9

3   2 → 5

6 → 3   3

5 → 8   3

4 → 2   2

Name ______________________________

Equivalence

Join those of equal value

Name ______________________________

Change

I spend	I pay	My change is
10p	20p	10p
12p	15p	
2p	5p	
11p	15p	
6p	7p	
3p	5p	
1p	5p	
4p	10p	
12p	20p	
14p	15p	
5p	10p	
7p	10p	
13p	20p	

Name ______________________

An add 5 rocket

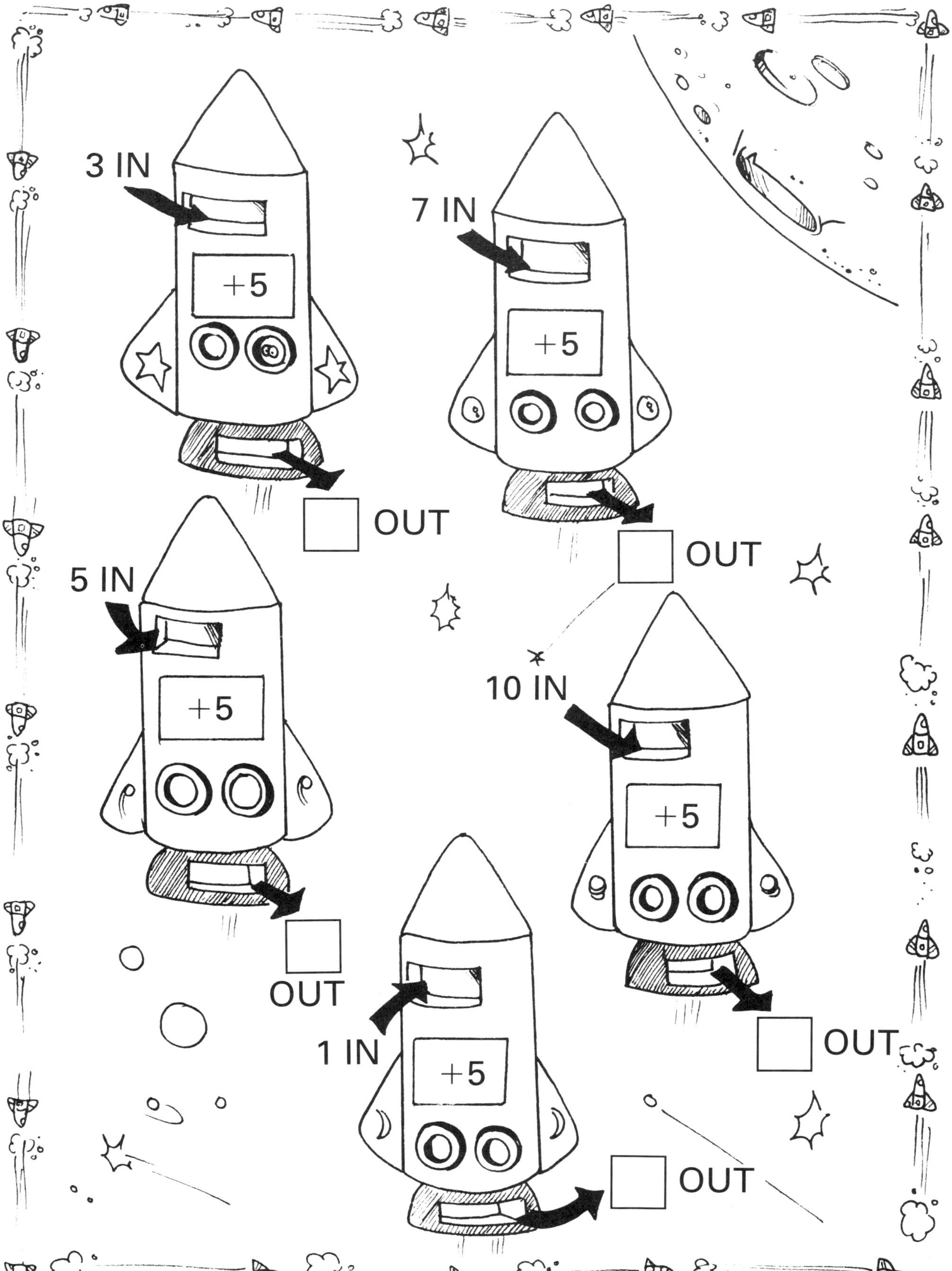

Name ______________________

A take away 7 machine

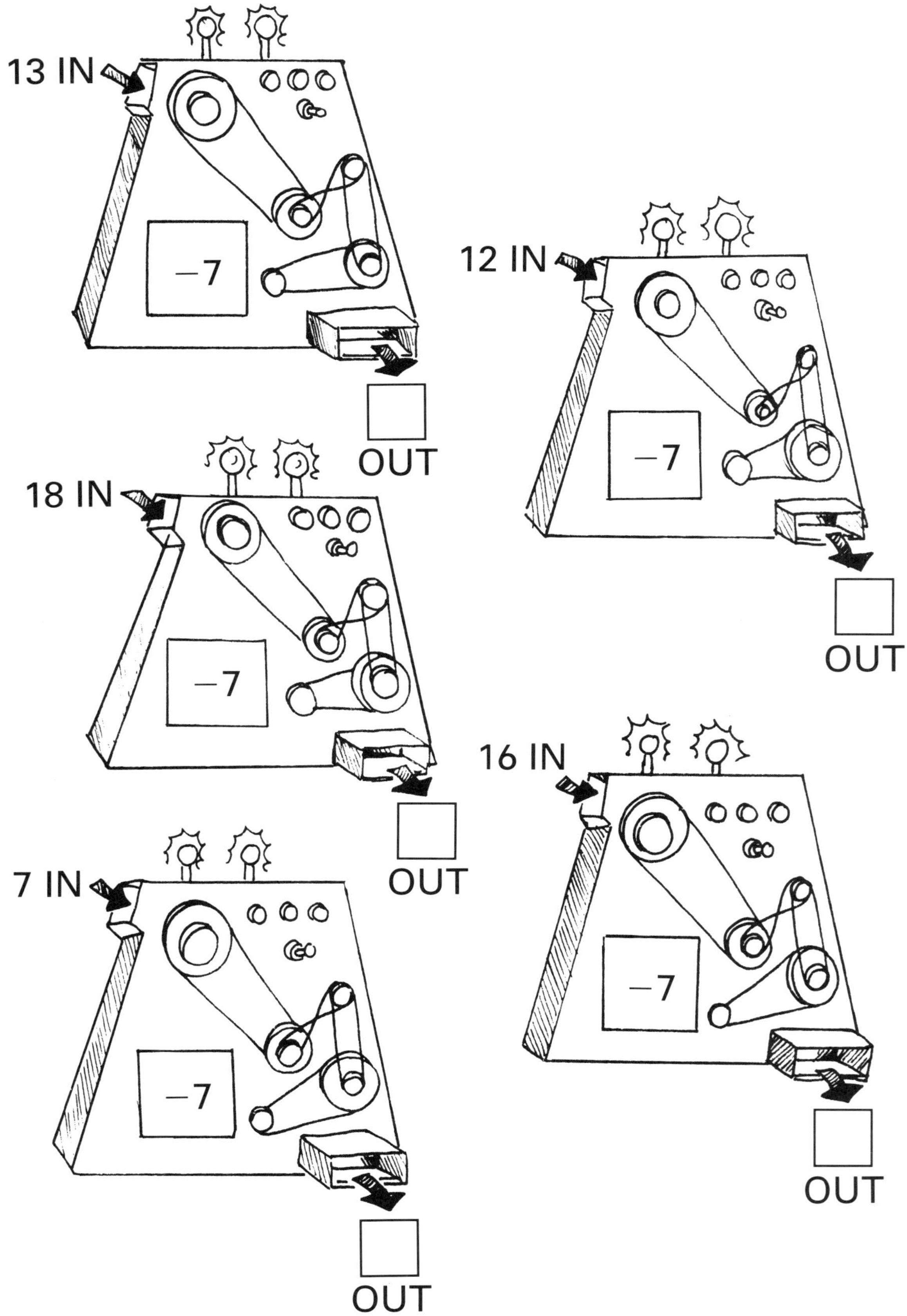

Name ______________________________

Star wars machines

Follow the trail

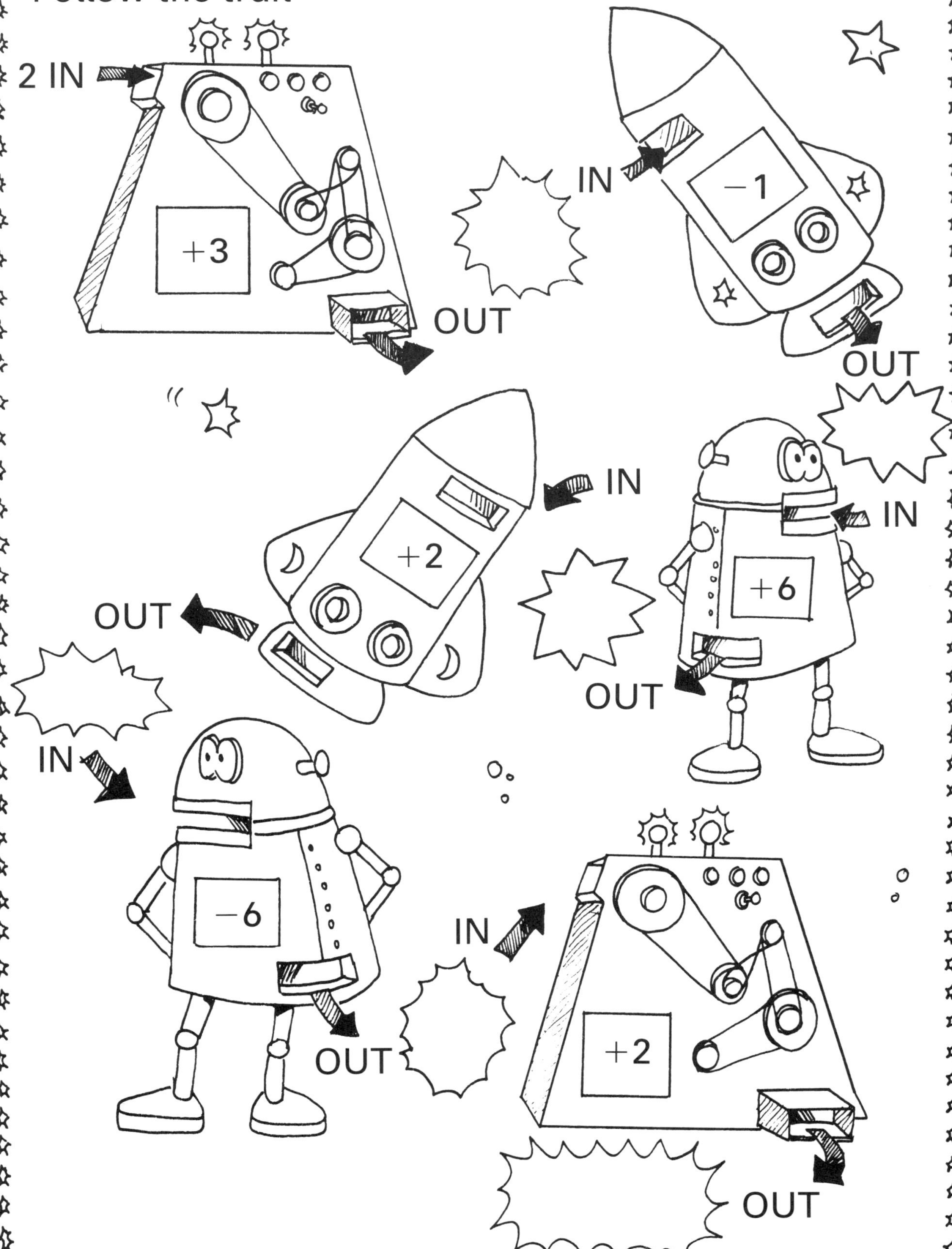

Name ______________________________

Mystery machines

What do these machines do?

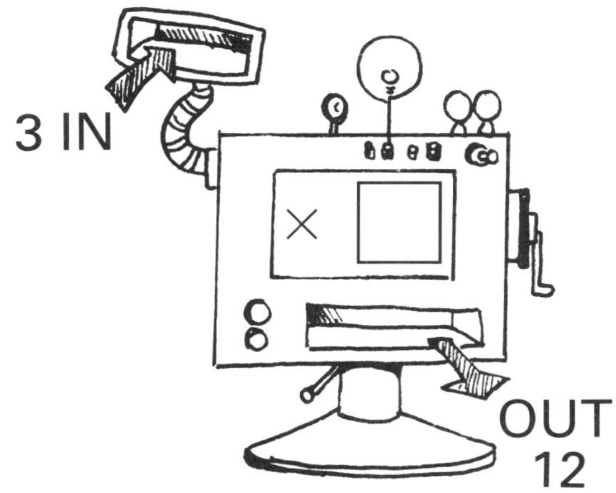

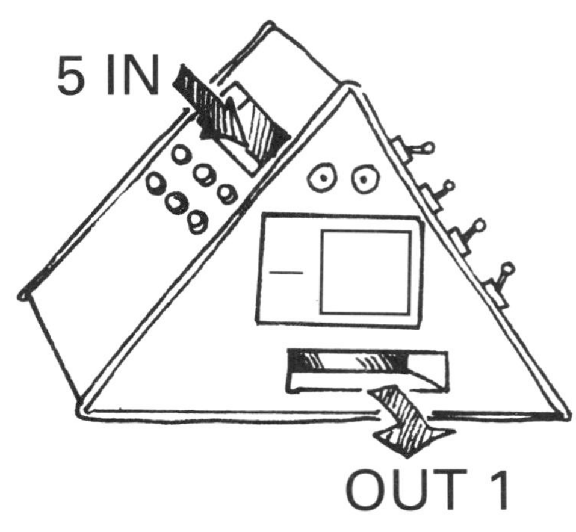

Name ______________________________

Choose how to compute

The problem	Is it + − × or ÷?	How to do it
 5 apples come off a tree and then 10 more. How many apples fall?		
 Cake comes in packs of 8 slices. How many slices in 5 packs?		
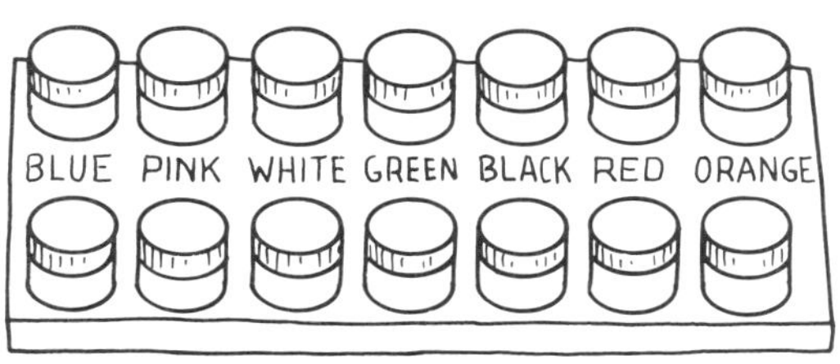 Paints come in packs like this. If all the red and black is used how many pots are left?		
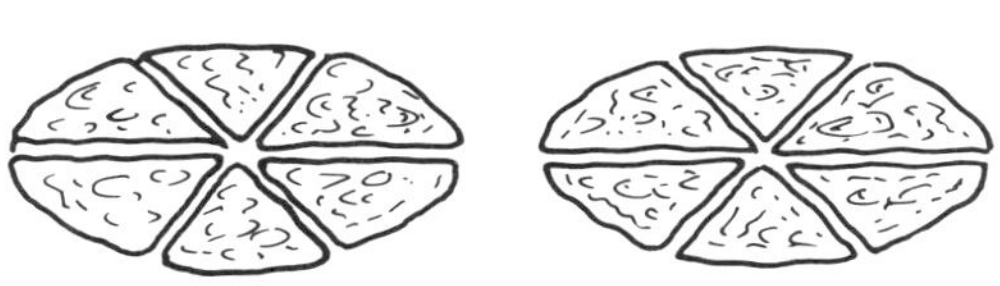 2 pizzas. Each in 6 pieces. How many people can have 3 slices each?		

Name ______________________________

Choose how to compute

The problem	Is it + − × or ÷?	How to do it
56 children are absent from a school with 203 pupils. How many are at school? 		
 How many toys in the lucky dip if 78 children can have 2 goes each?		
 There are 11 people in a cricket team. How many teams can be made from 60 people? 		
If 2 appears in half of all phone numbers, how many of 5438 phone numbers will have a 2 in them? 		
Here are the numbers of people who go to the zoo each day. How many in total? 74 39 41 89 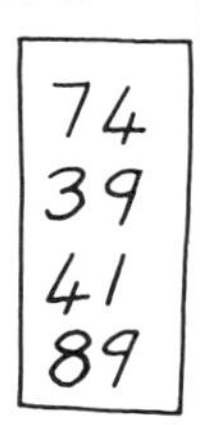		
An insect has 6 legs. How many legs on 60 insects?		

Name ______________________________

Tens and units: addition

		Answers
13 + 21		
25 + 62		
44 + 37		
90 + 9		
14 + 73		

Name ______________________

Tens and units: subtraction

		Answers
64 – 13		
75 – 22		
38 – 15		
99 – 41		
50 – 25		

Name ______________________________

Add and subtract with approximation steps

Work out rough answers
to these

41 + 31	
69 + 22	
78 − 32	
51 + 39	
29 + 48	
61 − 20	

Name ____________________

Mapping

Give each drink a straw

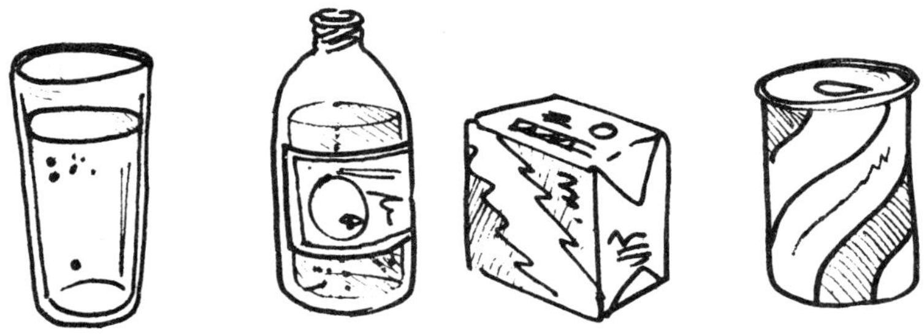

☐ drinks

☐ straws

Give each stick a toffee apple

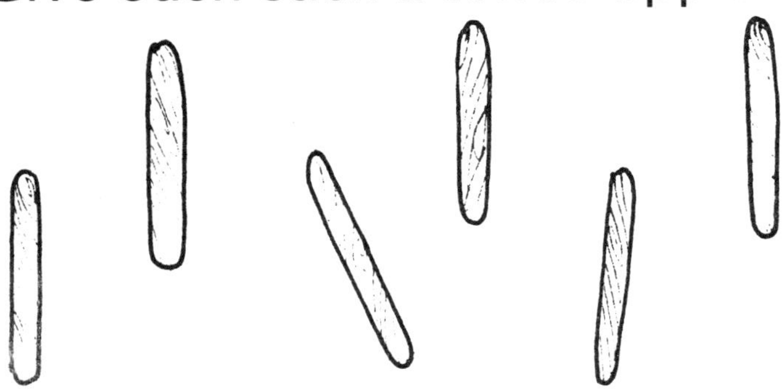

☐ sticks

☐ toffee apples

Give each woman a mouth

☐ women

☐ mouths

Give each kite a string

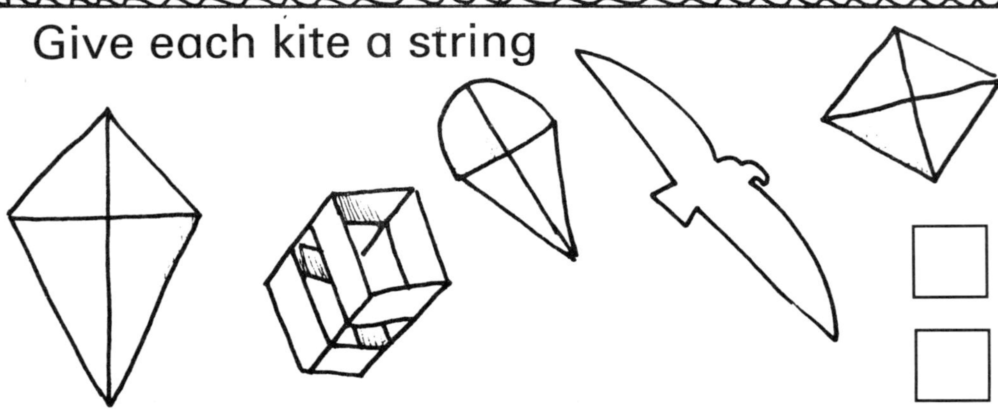

☐ kites

☐ strings

Name ____________________

Complex mapping

Match lambs to ewes

Match shoes to feet

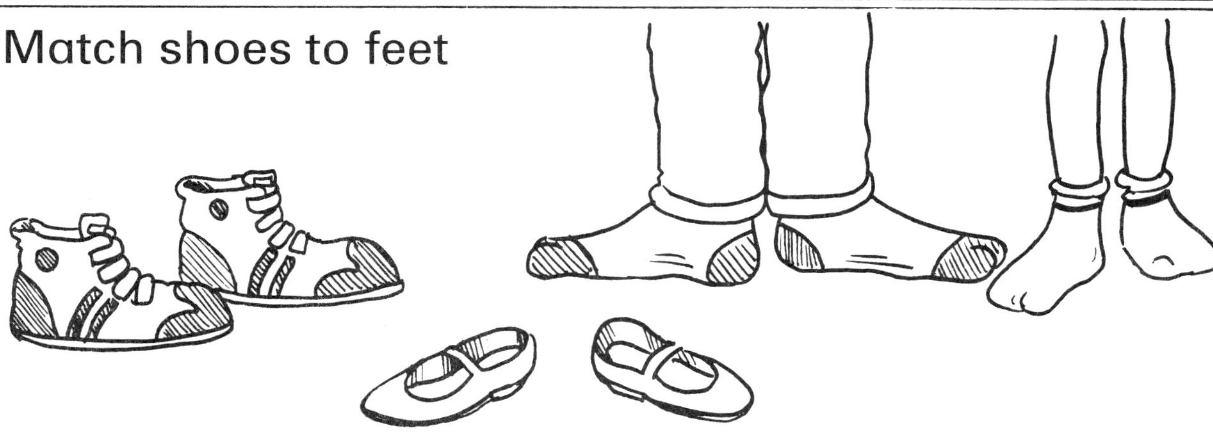

Match wheels to cars

Name ______________________________

Weather frequency table

Weather ... a 20 day study

Key

sunny day

cloudy day

rainy day

	||||
	||||||||||
	||||||

Name ______________________________

Frequency data collection

Key

What you are looking for

How many times it happens

Name ______________________

Customer frequency table

Day of week	Number of customers between 9 o'clock and 10 o'clock		
	TV	Flowers	Fruit
Monday	|	|||	||
Tuesday	||	|||||	||||
Wednesday	|||	||||	||||||
Thursday	|	||	||||||
Friday	|||||	||||||||||	||||||||||
Saturday	||||	||||||||	||||||||

Name ______________________

Graph axes and grid

Name ______________________________

Problem cards for block graphs or bar charts

Find out what your classmates' favourite meals are

Find out your classmates' shoe sizes

What pets do your classmates have?

Find out your classmates' favourite colours

Name ____________________

Shopping list and index

How many items are on the list? ☐

What comes after 'eggs'? ____________

What is the first item? ____________

What is the last item? ____________

Index to ____________ (Write in the title of your book)

What is the first word in the index? ____________

What is the first word under these letters?

M ____________ K ____________

E ____________ Y ____________

S ____________ D ____________

What is the last word in the index? ____________

What letters of the alphabet have *no* entries in the index? ____________

Name ______________________

Pictograms

How many girls in a class?

Key 6 girls

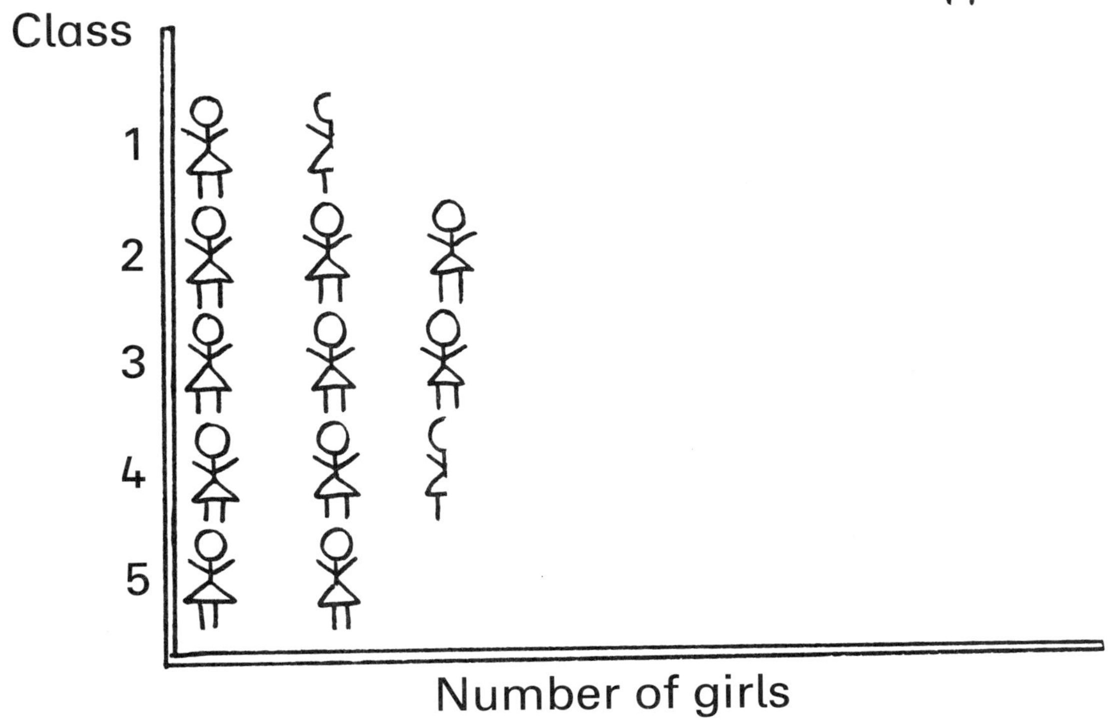

School meal preference

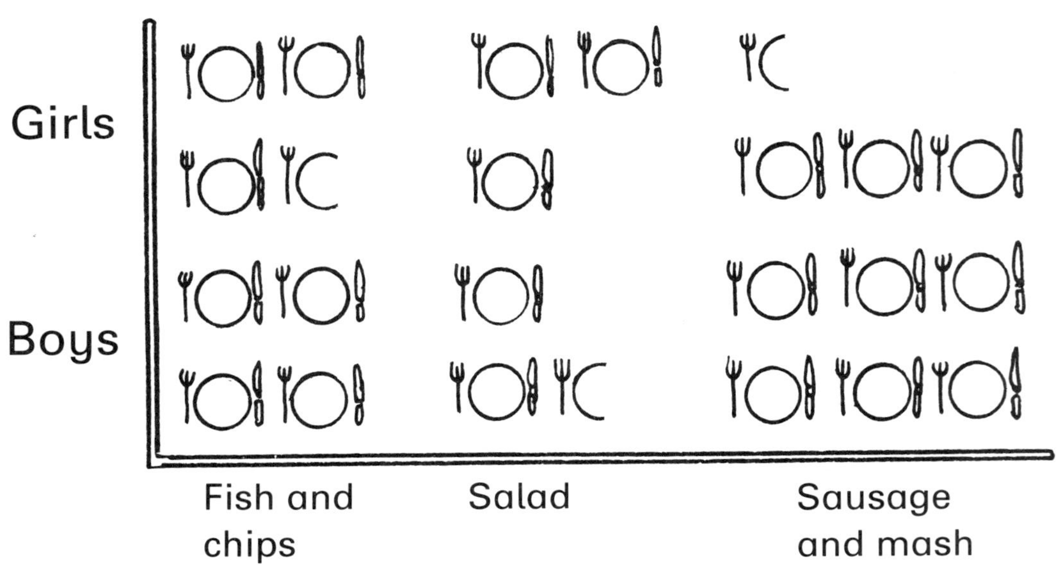

Key 10 meals

Name ______________________

Pictograms

Favourite cartoon characters

Key ☆ 2 people

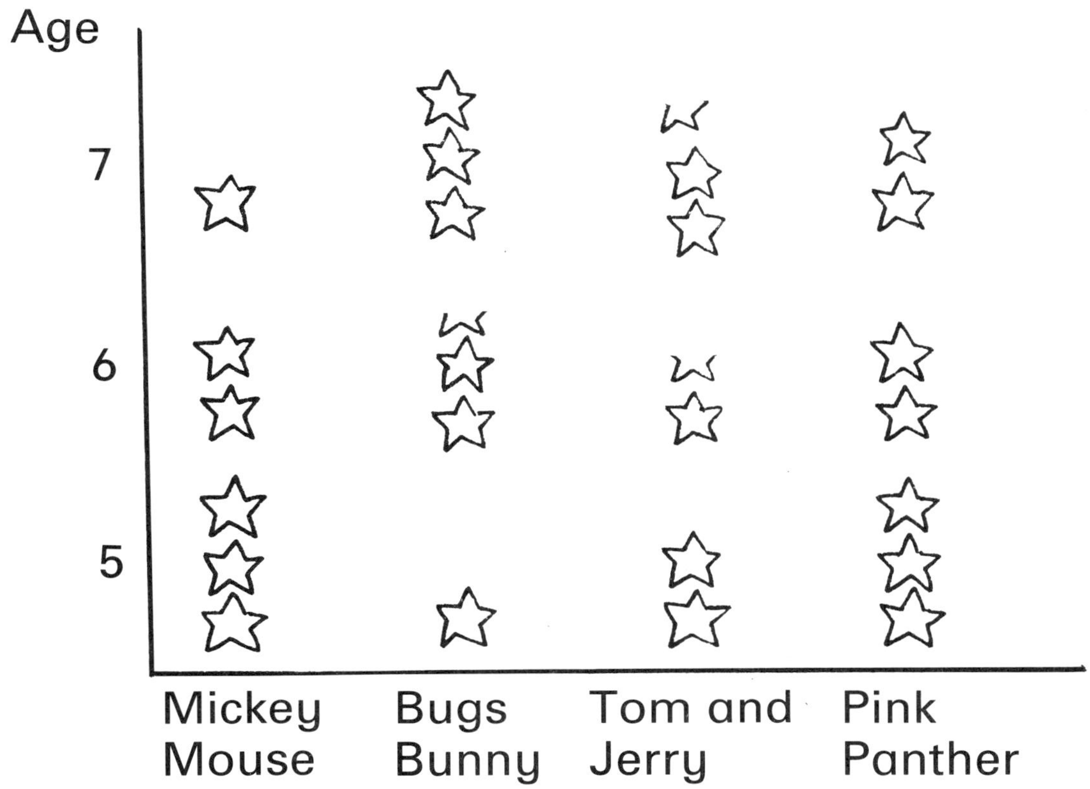

Does it rain more often on Mondays?

Key ☁ 2 days

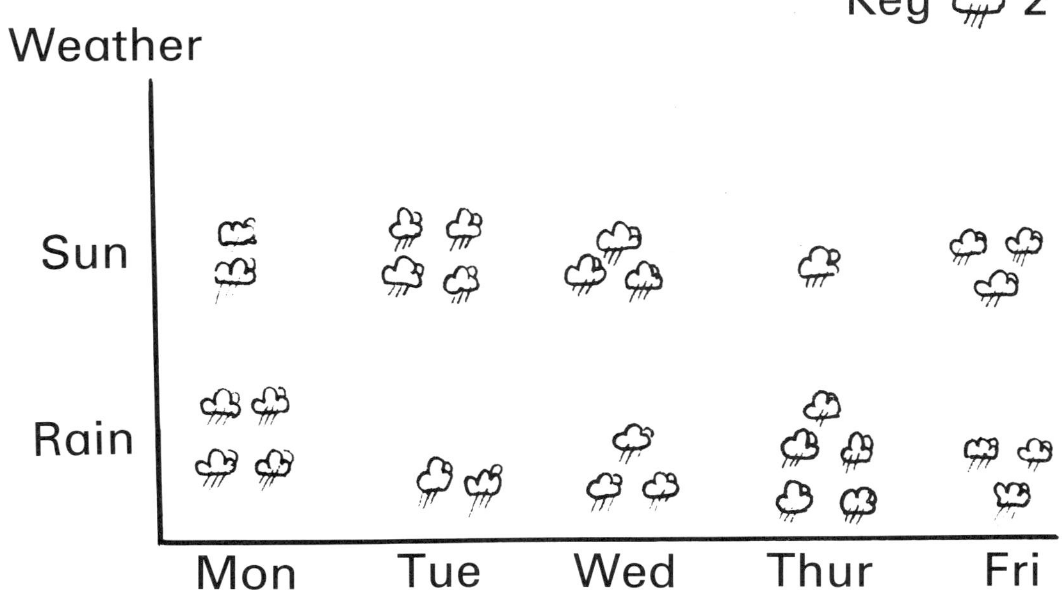

Name ______________________________

Shape pictures

Draw a man of ○ and ▭

Draw a kite of △

Draw a dog of □ and △

Draw a house of □ and ▭

Name ______________________

Shape match

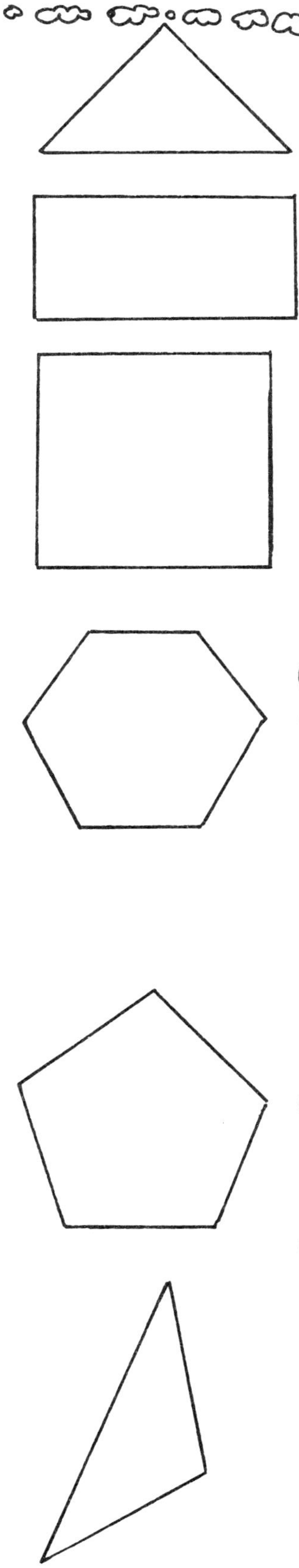

3 sides

triangle

5 sides

square

6 sides

pentagon

2 pairs of sides the same

4 corners the same

triangle

4 sides the same

4 corners the same

rectangle

3 sides

hexagon

Name ______________________________

Shape match – board

square	rectangle	hexagon	pentagon	triangle
4 sides	4 sides	6 sides	5 sides	3 sides
sides all same	pairs of sides same			
4 corners	4 corners			
corners all same	corners all same			

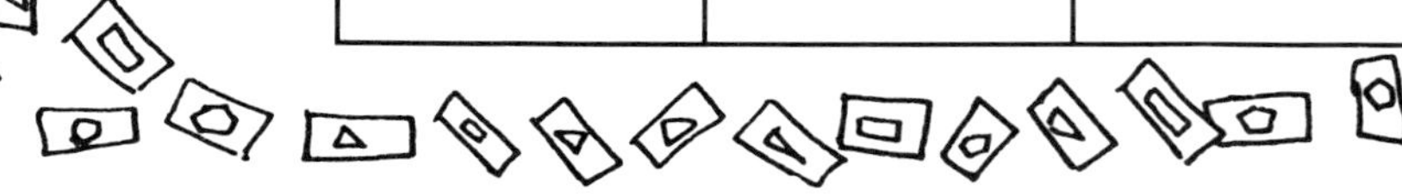

Name ______________________________

Shape match – cards

	square	4 sides	sides all same	4 corners	corners all same
	rectangle	4 sides	pairs of sides same	4 corners	corners all same
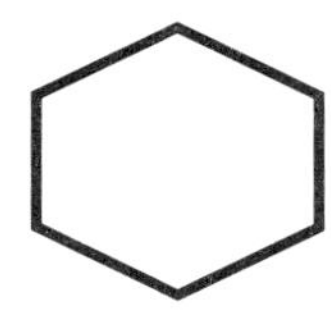	hexagon	6 sides			
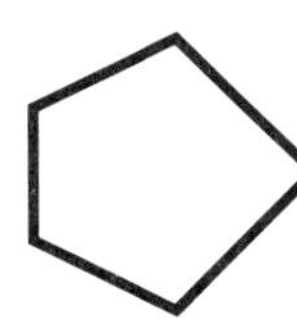	pentagon	5 sides			
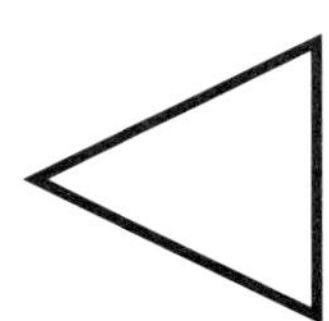	triangle	3 sides			

Name ______________________

Cubes and cuboids

These are all cuboids
Colour them
Ring the cubes

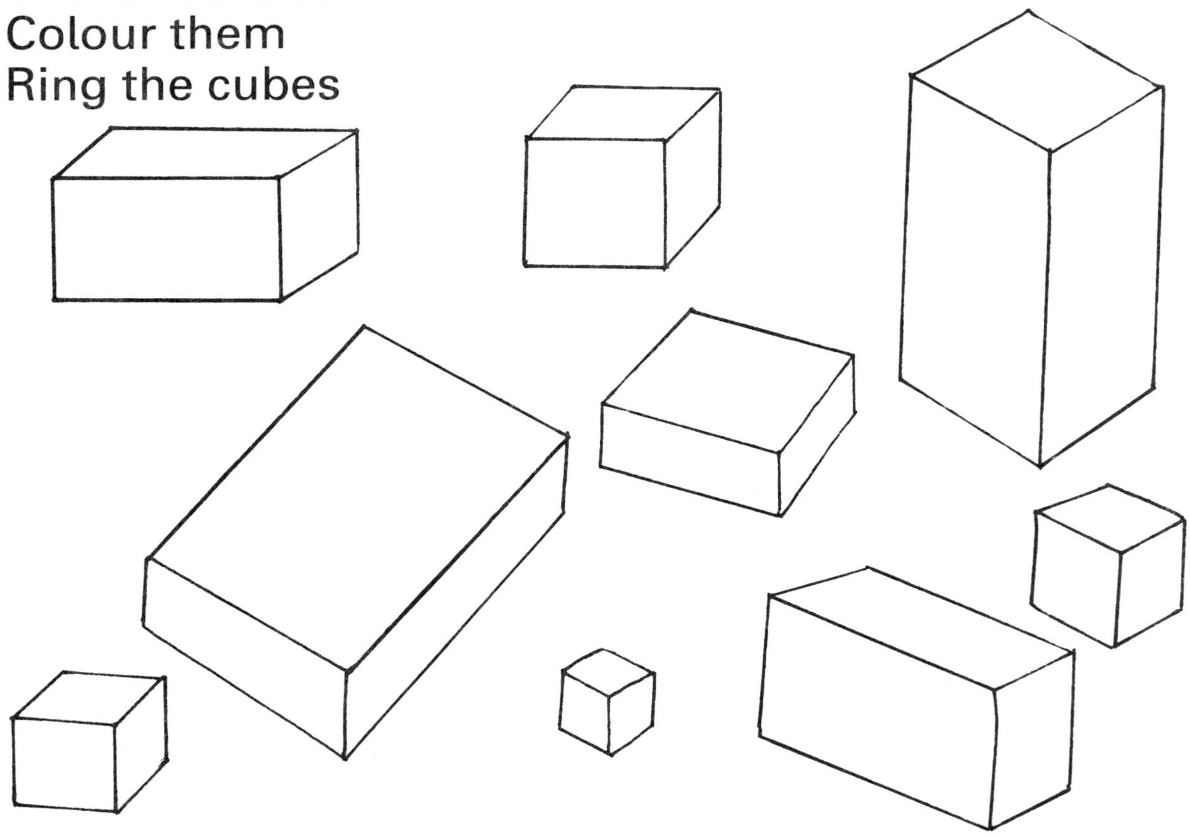

☑ Tick if true

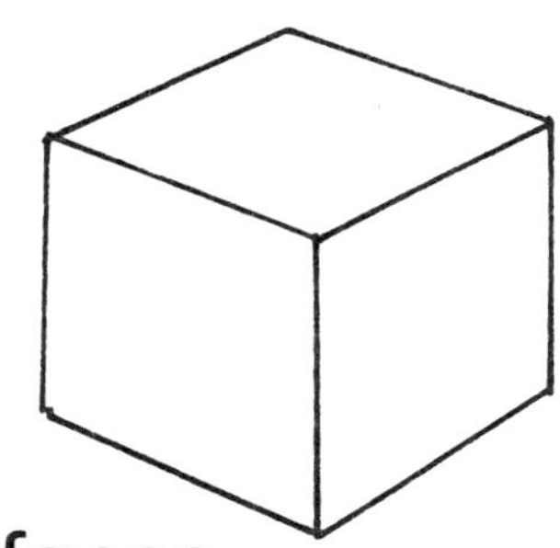

- ☐ 3 faces
- ☐ 12 edges
- ☐ Faces all different
- ☐ Faces all the same
- ☐ 4 faces
- ☐ 6 faces
- ☐ Corners all the same

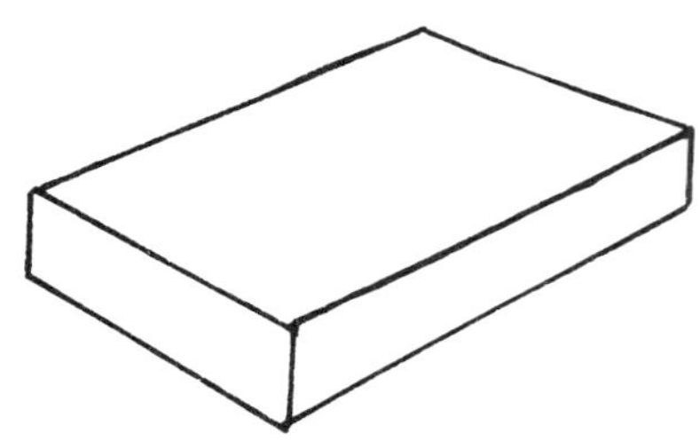

- ☐ Faces all the same
- ☐ Matching pairs of faces
- ☐ 4 faces
- ☐ 6 faces
- ☐ Corners all different
- ☐ Corners all the same

Name ____________________

Cylinders

Draw a cylinder

Draw a cylinder cut open and laid flat

Colour the cylinders

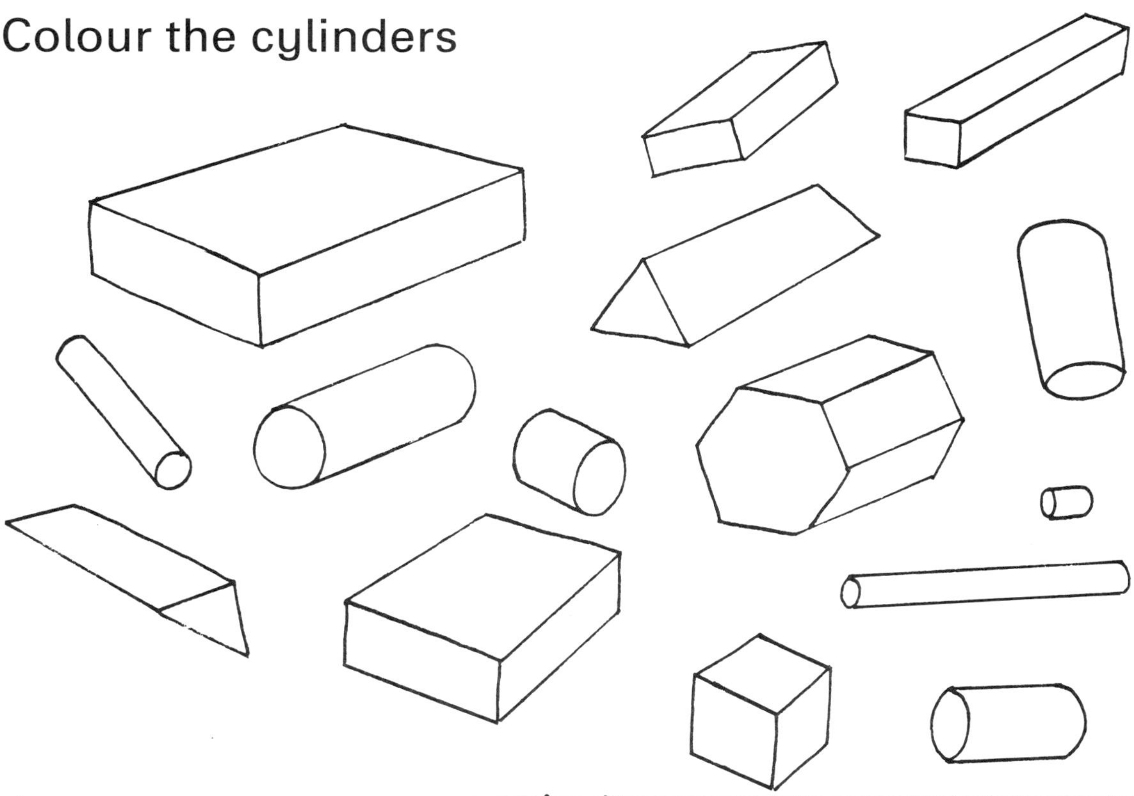

Name ______________________________

3-D shape game – base boards

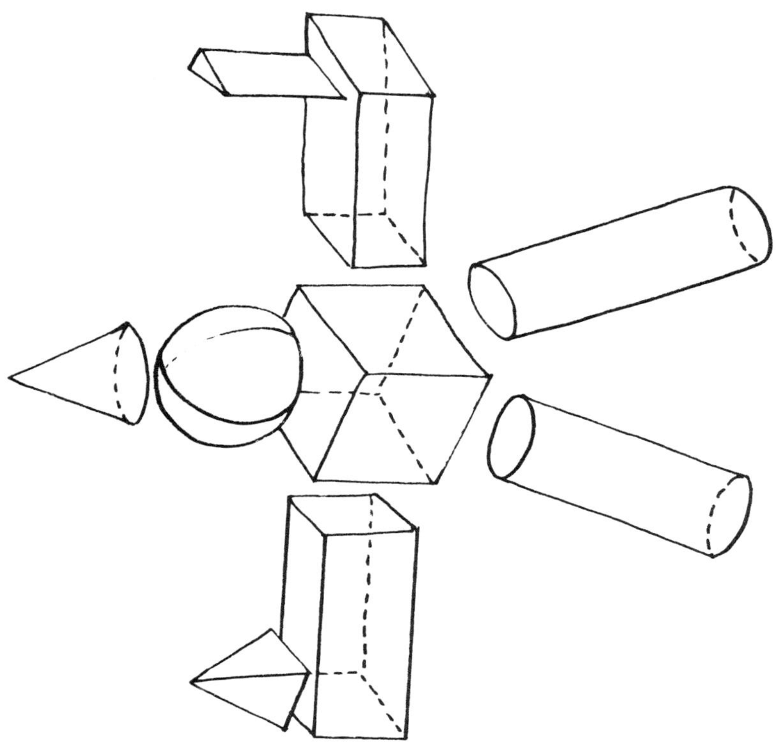

Collect 9 shape cards
to make this model

cuboid – 2 cube – 1
sphere – 1 cylinder – 2
triangular prism – 1
cone – 1 pyramid – 1

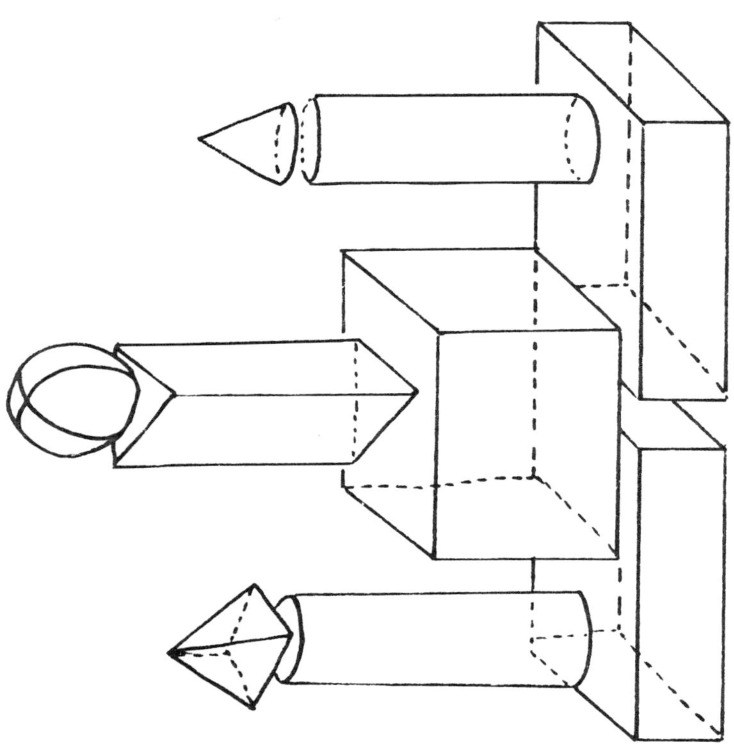

Collect 9 shape cards
to make this model

cuboid – 2 cube – 1
sphere – 1 cylinder – 2
triangular prism – 1
cone – 1 pyramid – 1

Name ______________________________

3-D shape game – base boards

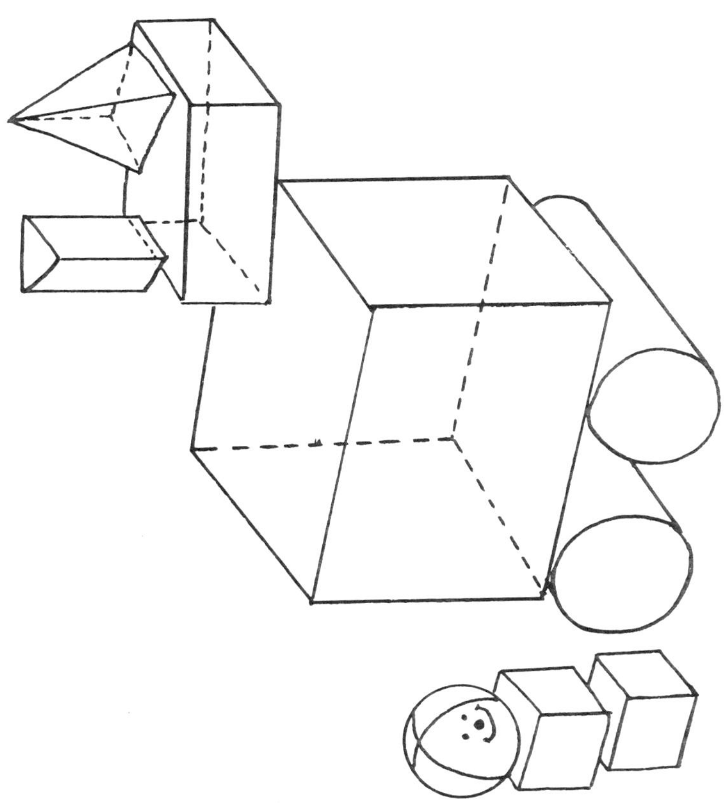

Collect 9 shape cards
to make this model

cuboid – 2 cube – 2
sphere – 1 cylinder – 2
triangular prism – 1
pyramid – 1

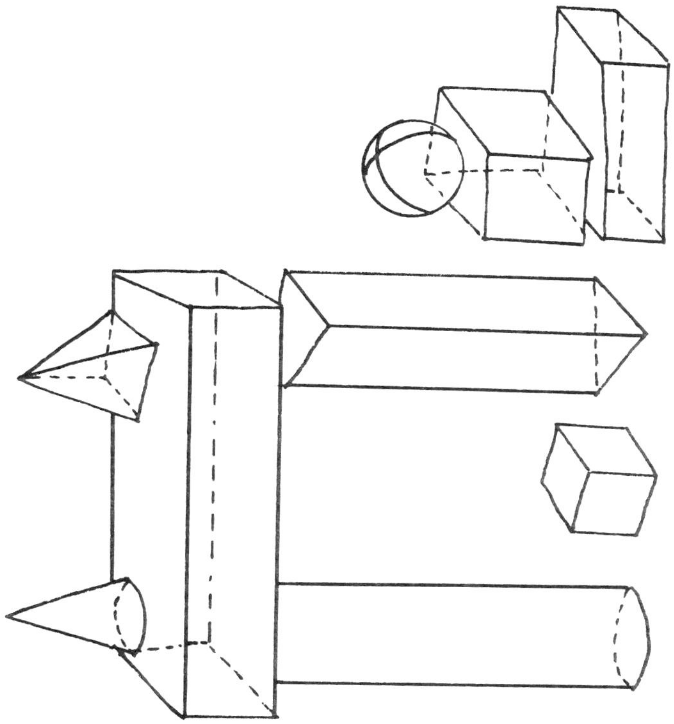

Collect 9 shape cards
to make this model

cuboid – 2 cube – 2
sphere – 1 cylinder – 1
triangular prism – 1
cone – 1 pyramid – 1

Name ______________________________

3-D shape game – cards

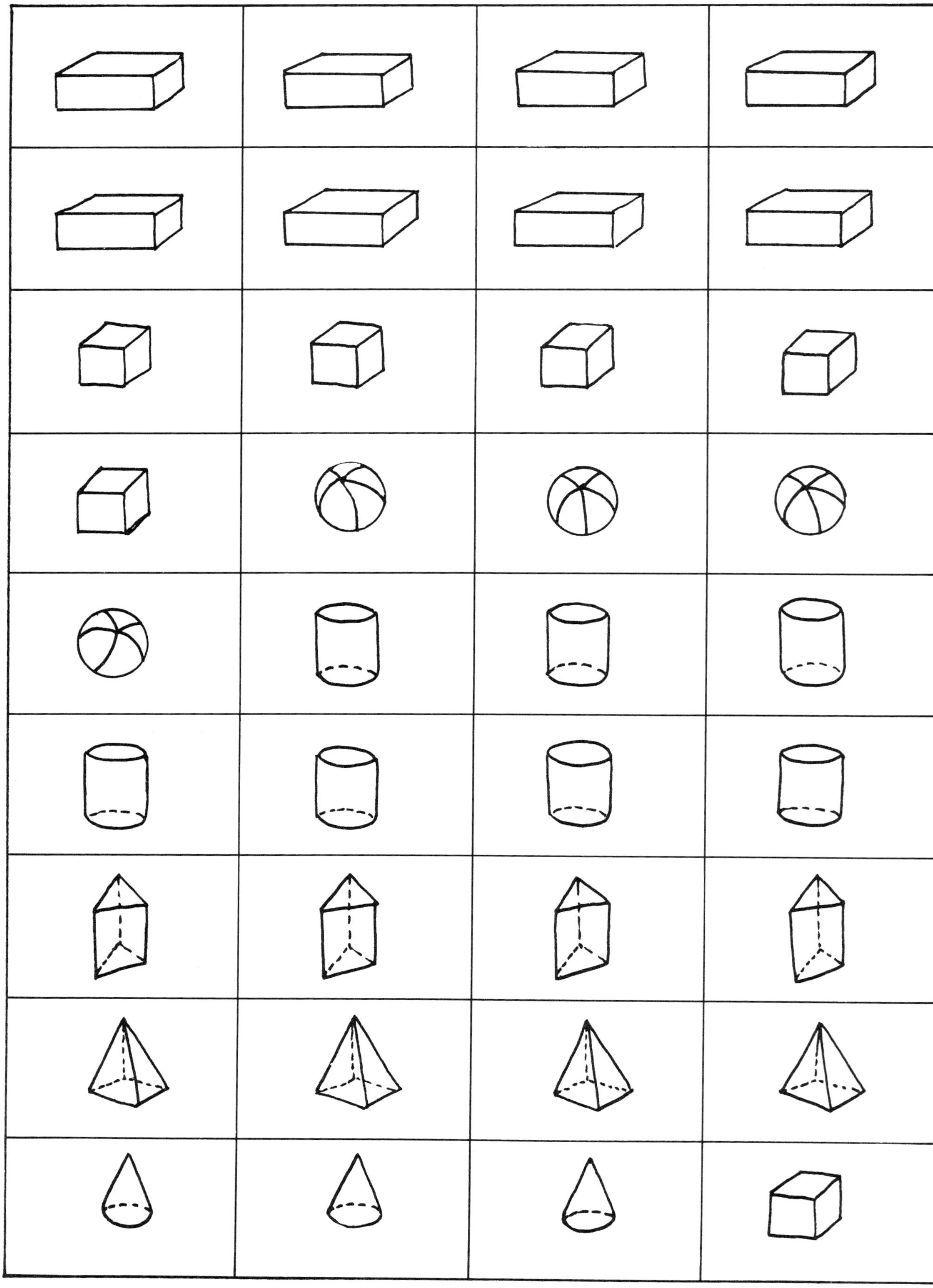

Name ______________________

2-D shapes quiz

What can you say about a triangle?

____

____

Name the shape with 6 sides ______________________

What shape has 4 sides the same and 4 corners the same? ______________________

Name this shape ______________________

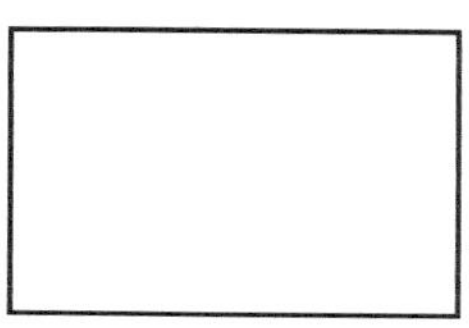

What shape has 5 sides? ______________________

Name this shape ______________________

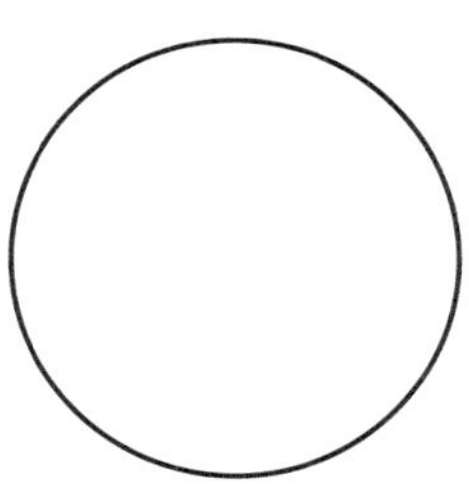

circle rectangle hexagon pentagon square

Name ______________________________

3-D shapes quiz

A die is a __________

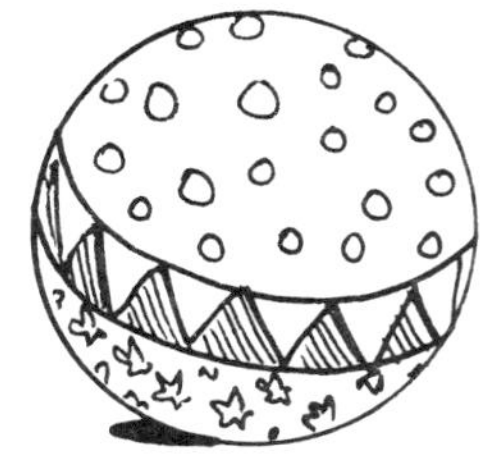

A ball is a __________

Telescopes are shaped like ____________________

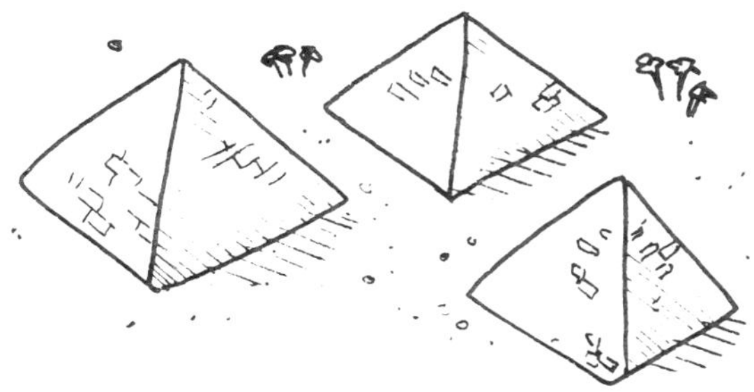

The Egyptians built the ____________________

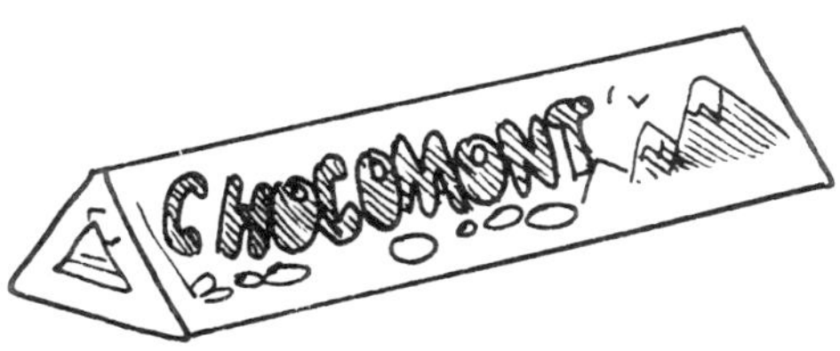

This shape is a

____

This shape is a

____

This shape is a

____

This shape is a ______________

cuboid	cube	triangular prism	cone	sphere	hexagonal prism
		pyramid	cylinder		

Name ______________________________

2-D shapes and symmetry

Colour the symmetrical shapes

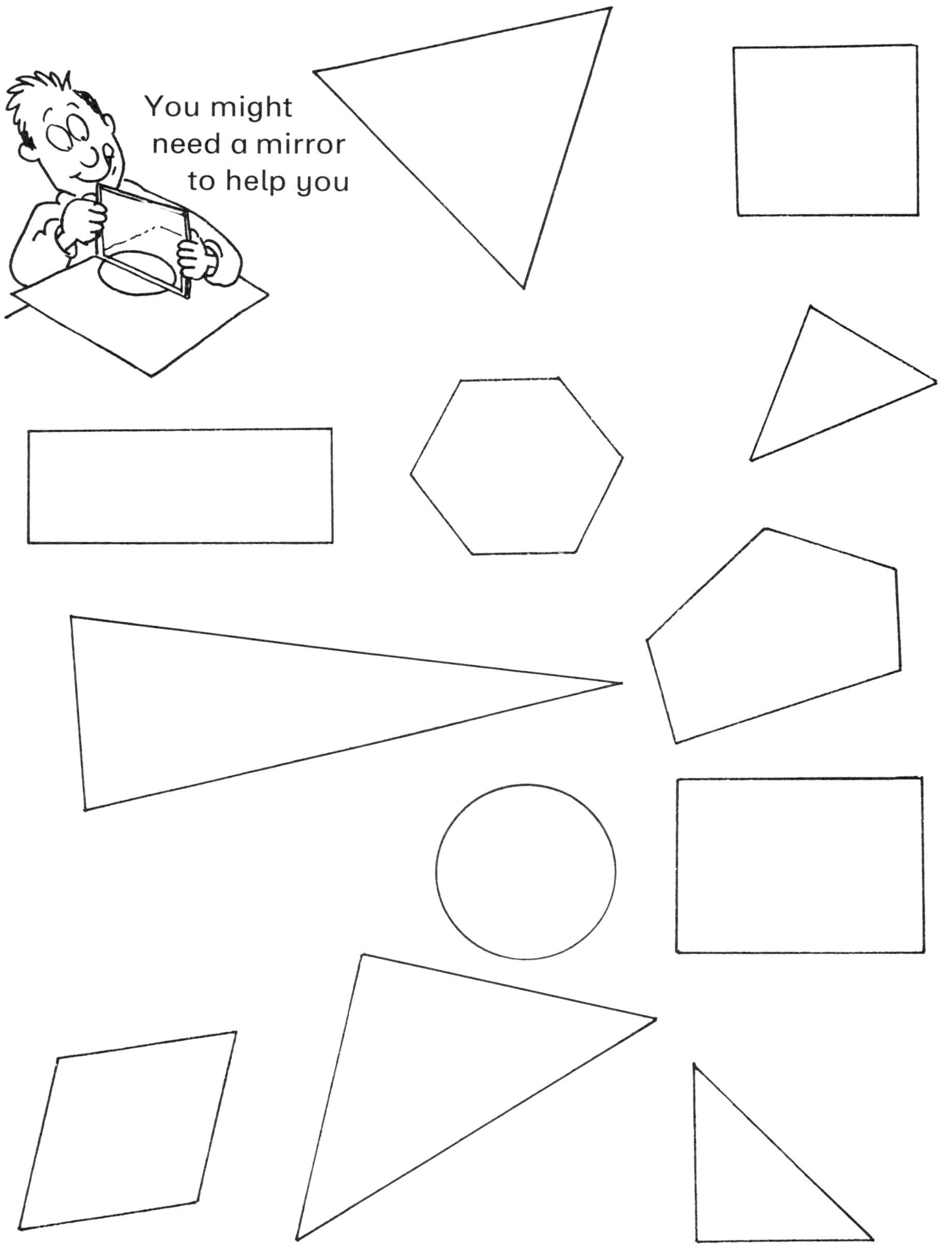

Name ______________________________

House number symmetry

The number on ________________ house is ________

Draw the number again. Make the number so big it nearly fills the page!

Check the numerals

Are they symmetrical?

Name ____________________

Letter symmetry

My name is ____________________

Draw your name, making the letters large
Tick the letters that are symmetrical

Name ____________________

Planes of symmetry

Write in how many planes of symmetry each shape has

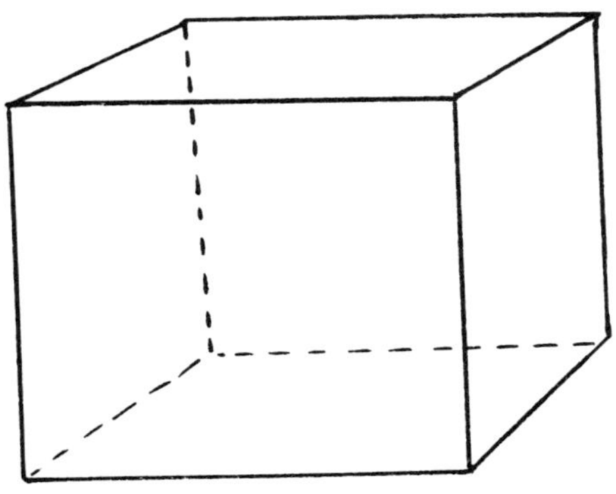

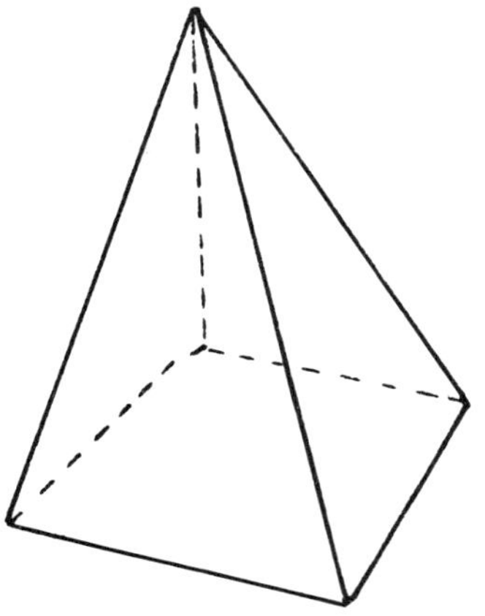

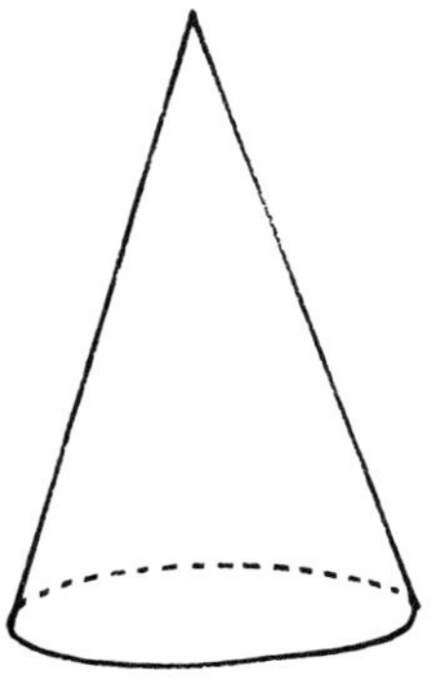

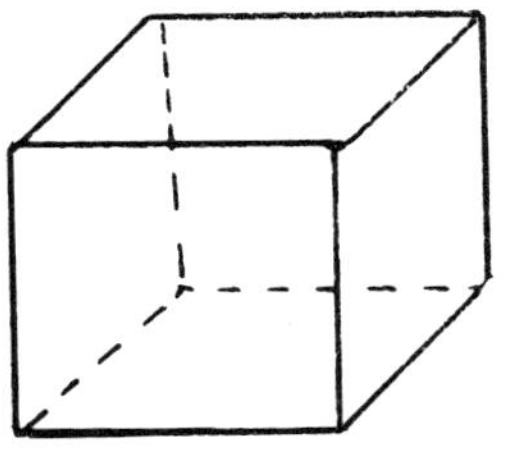

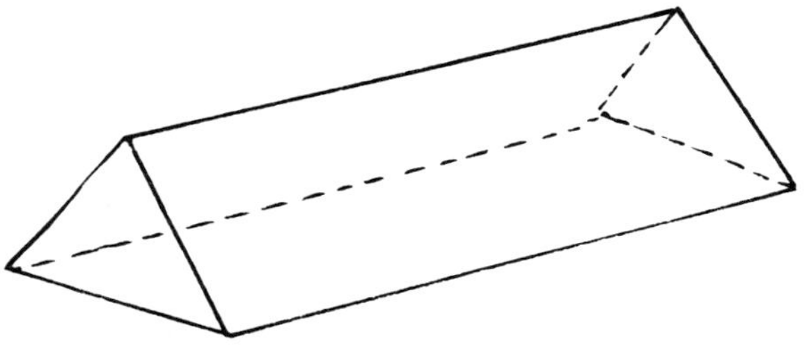

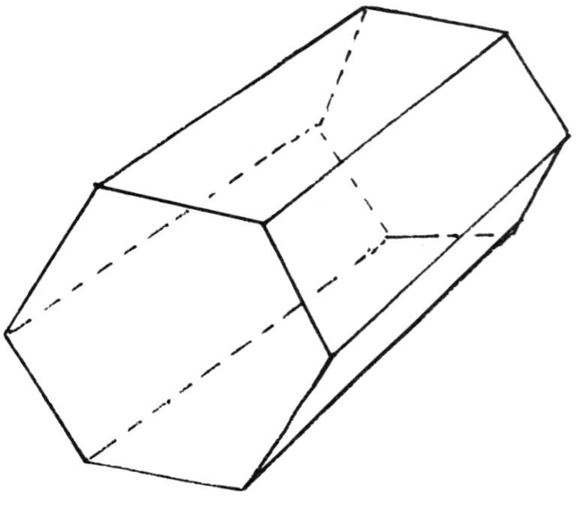

Name ______________________________

Position words

Ring the correct words

under / on

over / down

under / up

down / above

beside / above

on / under

beside / on

up / in front of

behind / over

on / down

above / under

Name ______________________________

Right angles

Draw the things you see with right angles

Mark the right angles

Name ______________________

Shapes with right angles

Circle the right angles

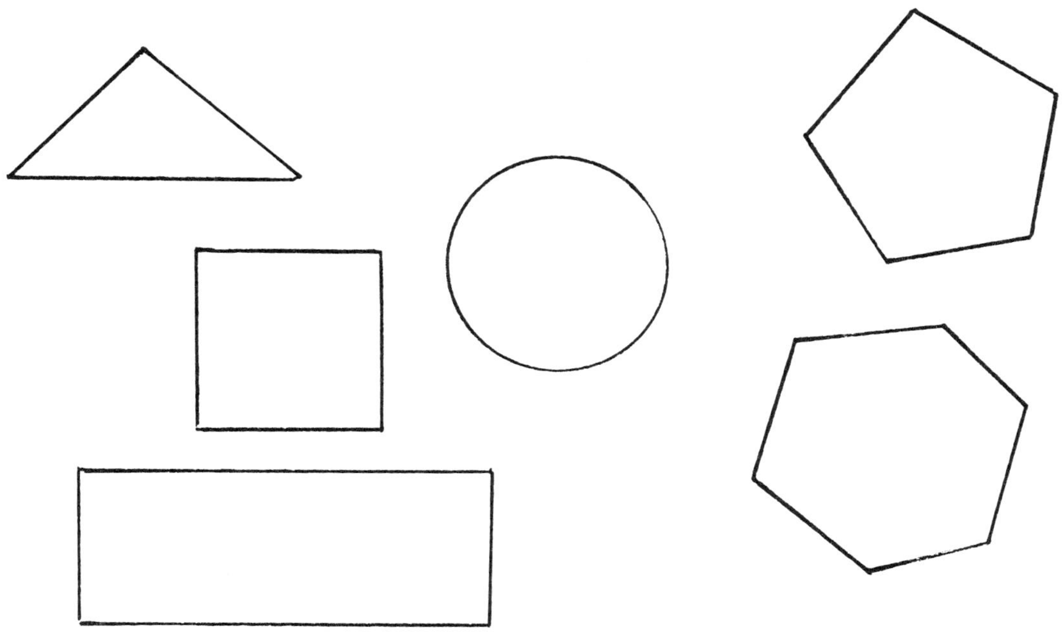

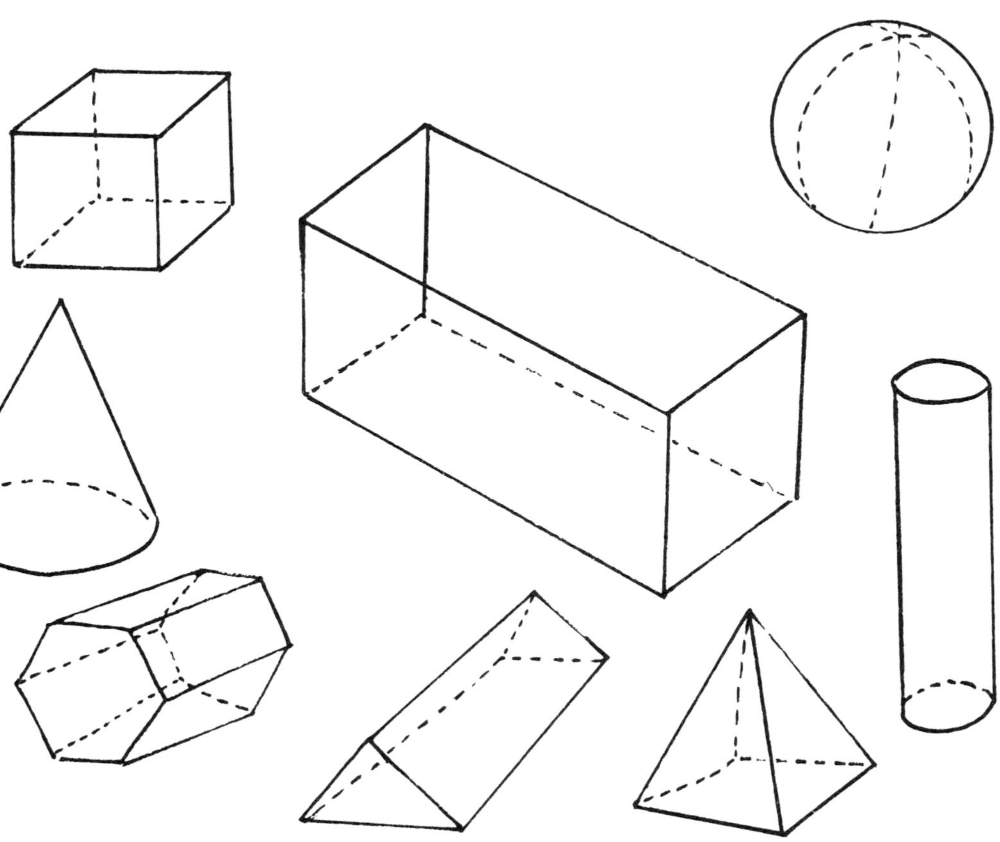

Name ______________________________

Angles around school

Look for angles like these	Where are they? Draw or write

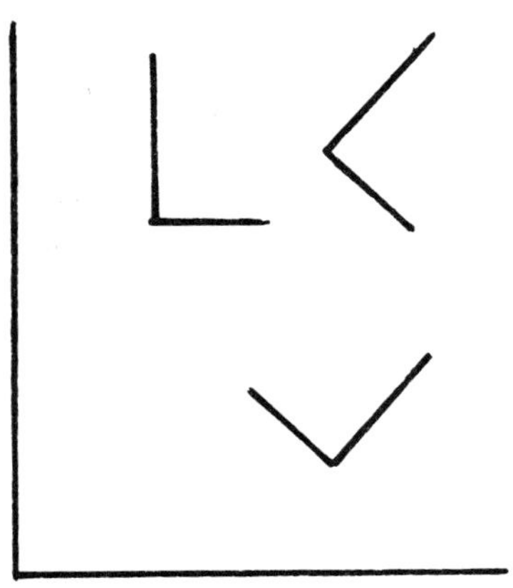	
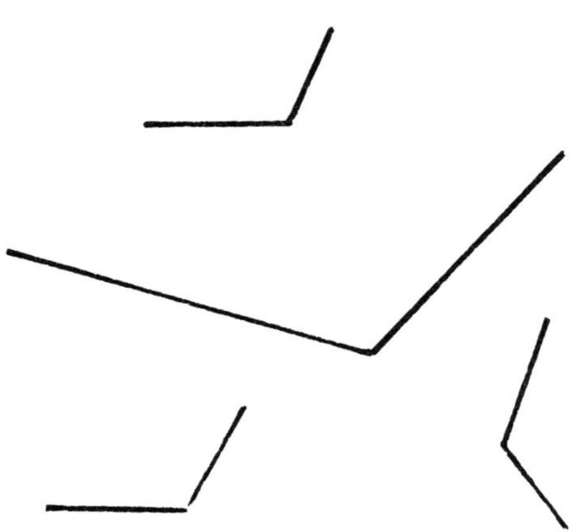	

Name ______________________________

Shape characters and play titles

Make up your own characters

What can you call your play?

The Shape Family goes Camping
or
Mr Cube's Bad Day
or ...

Draw your shape family here

Name ______________________

Measuring vocabulary

Ring these

2 4 6

Highest number

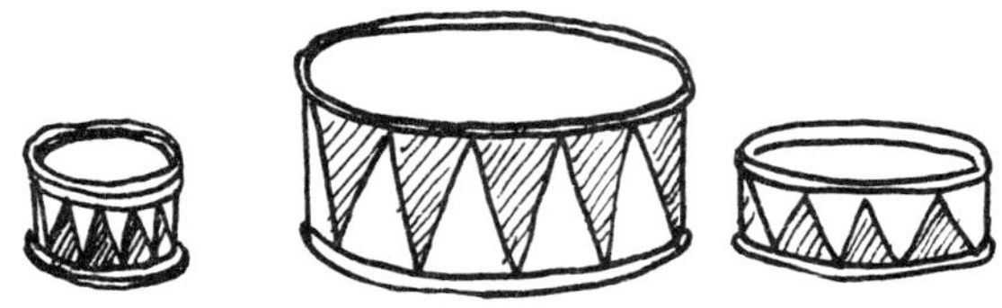

Smallest drum

Youngest child

Biggest door

Lightest

Fattest fish

Name ____________________

Comparing measurements

Draw yourself and two friends

Me	My friend	My friend
____________	____________	____________

Draw and write.

Hand ____________ has the biggest hand.

Coat ____________ has the biggest coat.

Pet/Toy ____________ has the smallest pet/toy.

Name ______________________________

Restaurant comments

Draw what you ate and drank

Write about the food

Name ______________________________

Exciting things to measure with

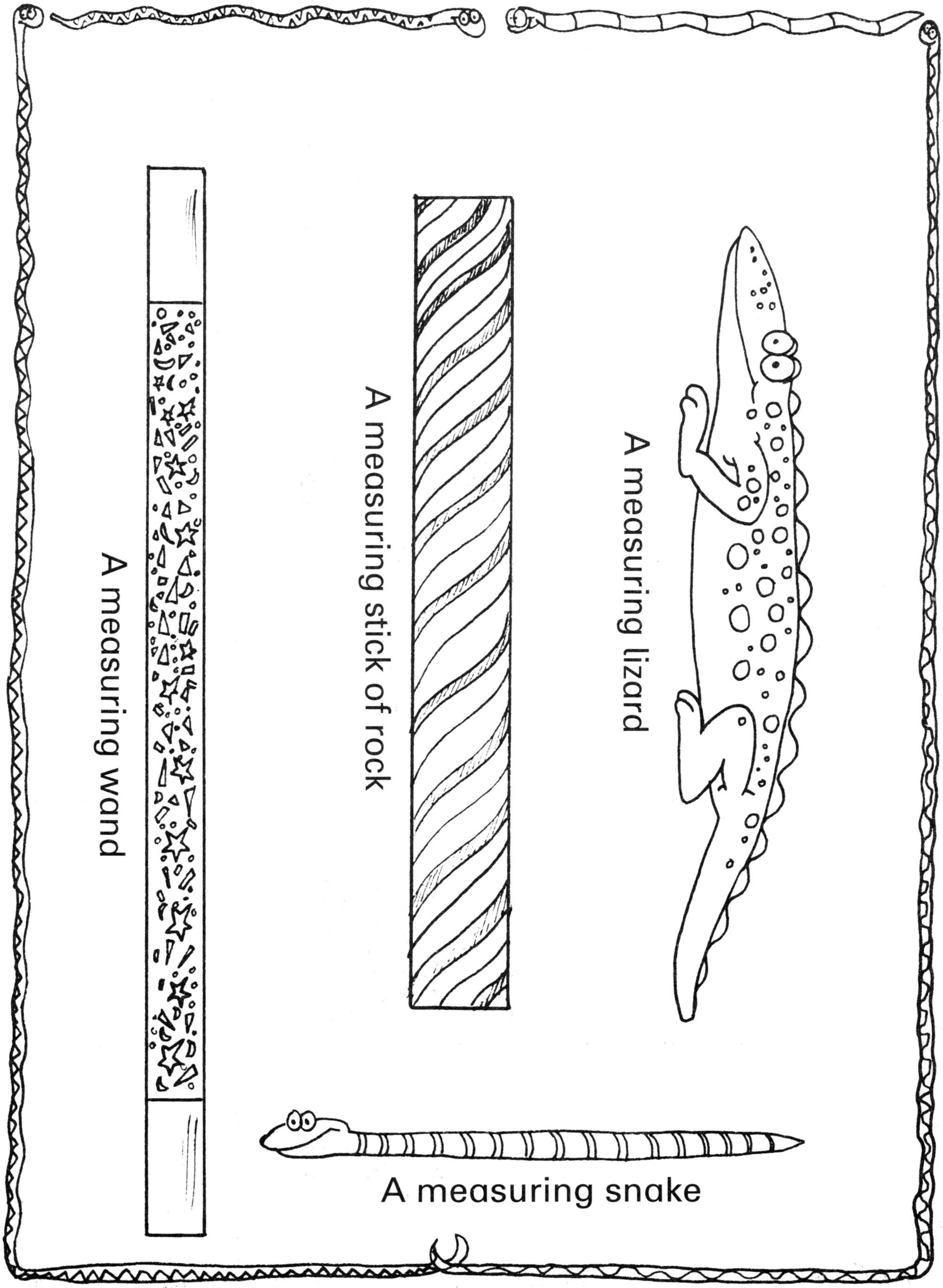

Name ______________________________

Measuring: non-standard units

Draw what you measure	Measure with:	How many?
	handspans 	
	strides 	
	thumbs 	
	books 	
	pencils 	

Name ______________________________

Capacity

Get four containers of different sizes

Label them

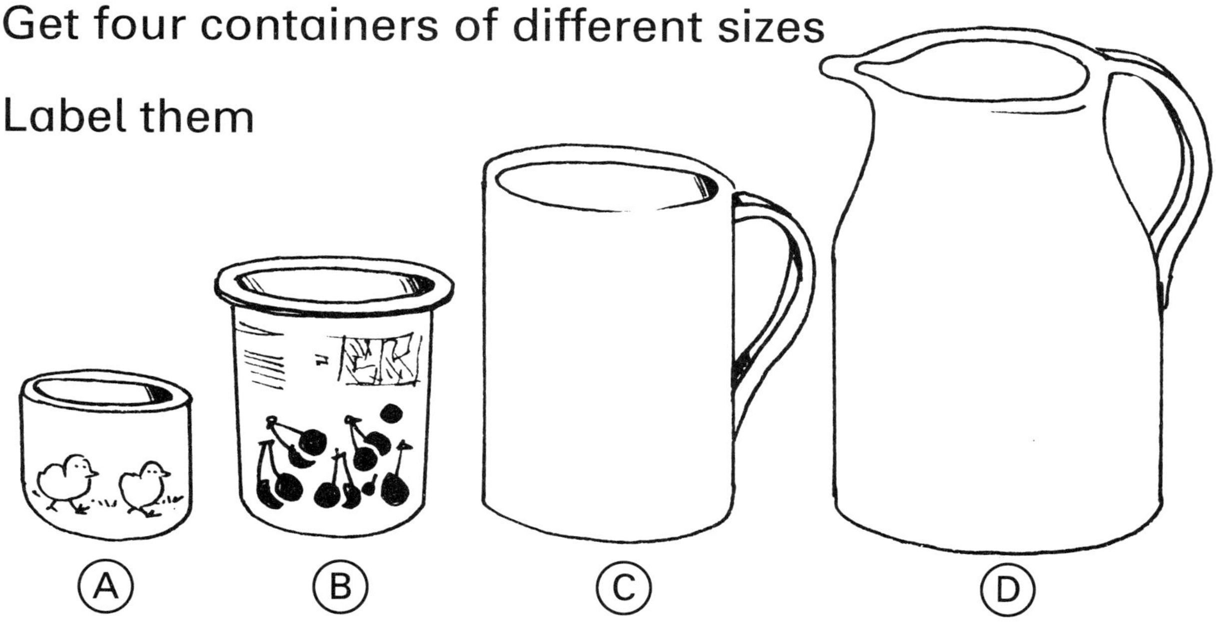

How many?

☐	(A) fill 1 (B)	☐	(B) fill 1 (C)
☐	(A) fill 1 (C)	☐	(B) fill 1 (D)
☐	(A) fill 1 (D)	☐	(C) fill 1 (D)

Do some more using another container

Name ________________________________

Measuring in centimetres

Measure in centimetres

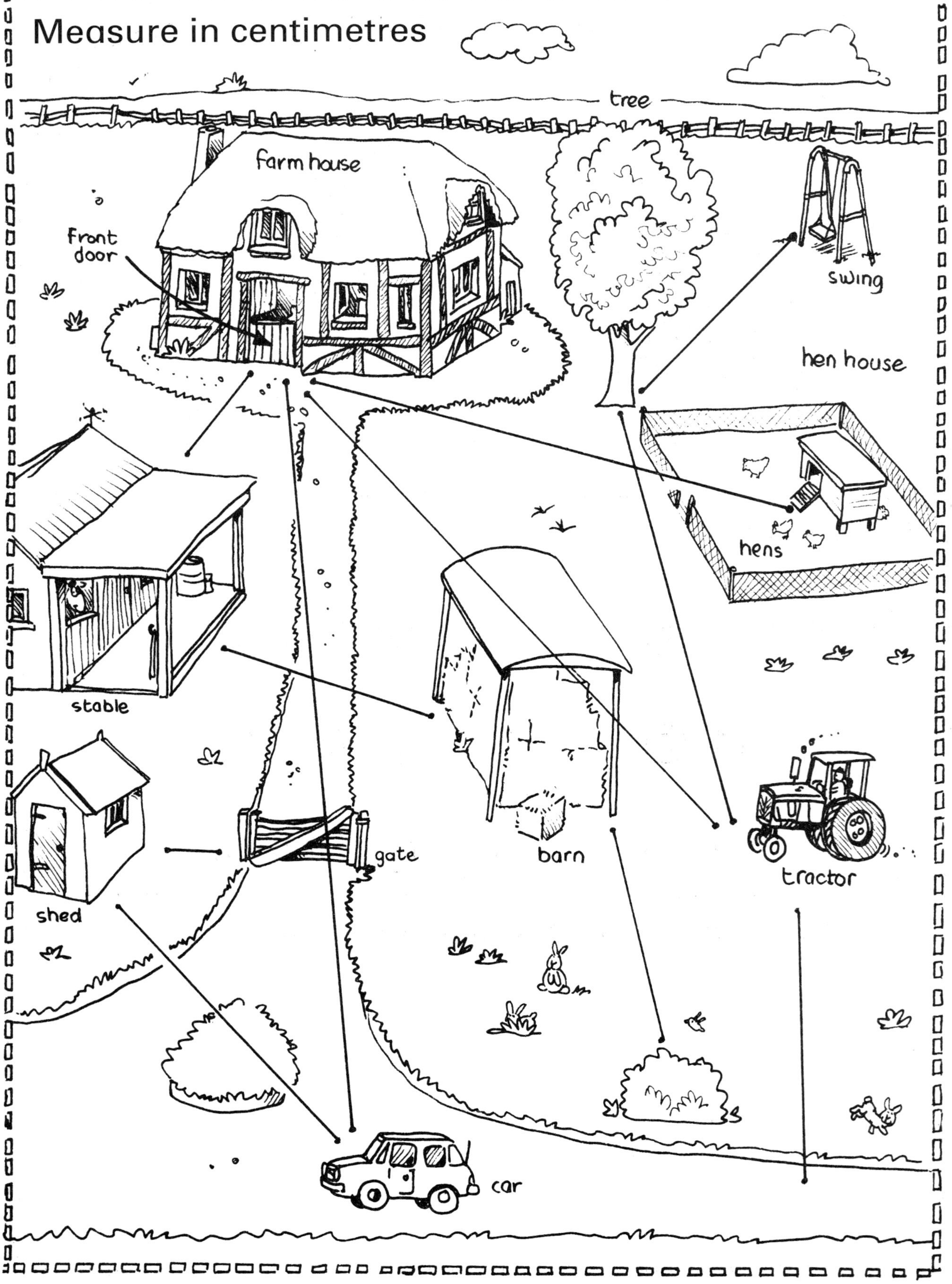

Name ____________________

Litres and millilitres

There are _____ millilitres in a litre.

A cup full of tea has _____ ml.

A milk bottle holds _____ ml.

Find some more containers.
Draw them and write on the drawings what they hold.

Name ___________________________

Clock face

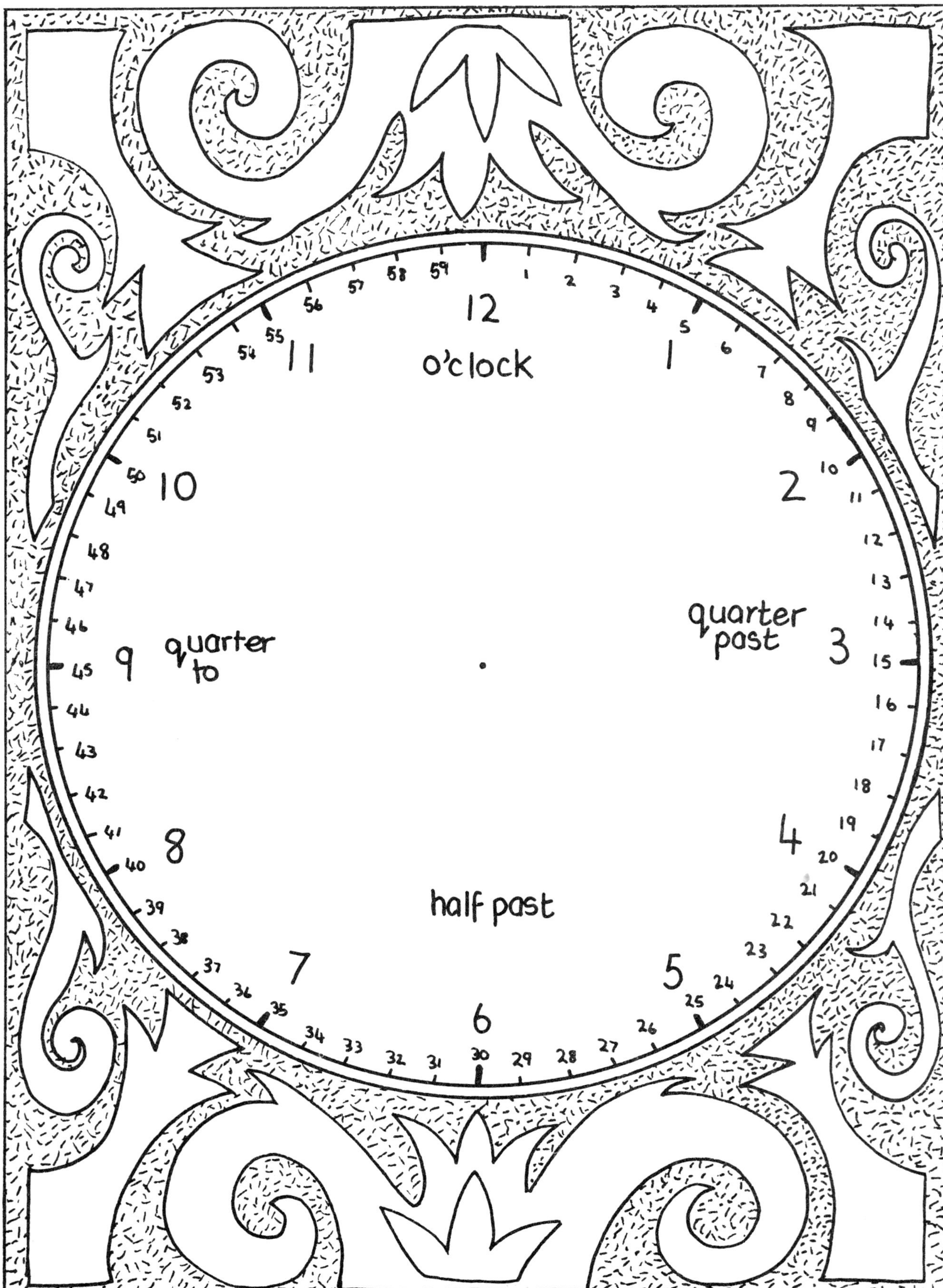

Name ______________________

Telling the time

What is the time?

The long hand has fallen off these clocks.
Can you still tell the time?

What time will these clocks show 1 hour later?

Name ______________________________

Digital/written time

Turn these into digital times

four o'clock

:

half past two

:

quarter past ten

:

quarter to one

:

Write these times in words

4:45 ____________________

12:10 ____________________

3:30 ____________________

11:00 ____________________

5:05 ____________________

10:15 ____________________

6:17 ____________________

Name ____________________

Time

Put in the hands

5 o'clock

9 o'clock

Write in the tin

______ ______ ______

What is the difference in time between these clocks?

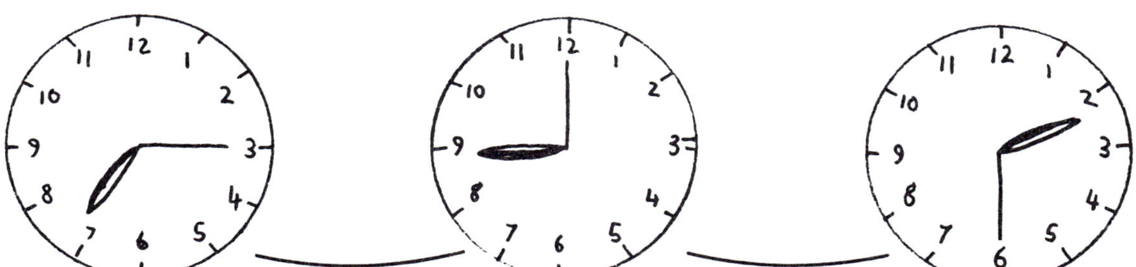

______ ______

The long hand has fallen off. What is the time?

______ ______ ______

Name ______________________

Spinners

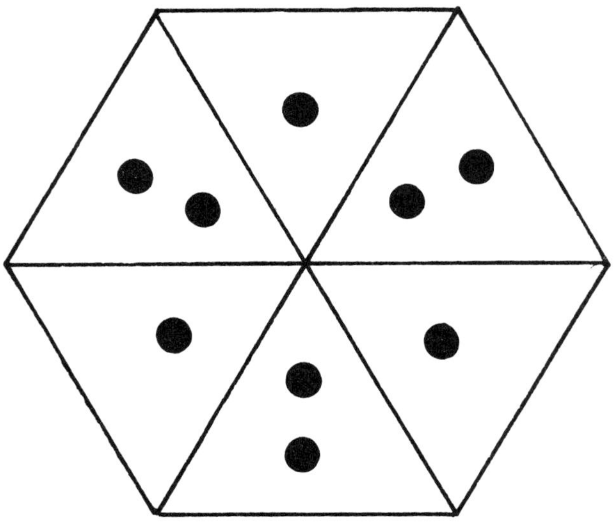

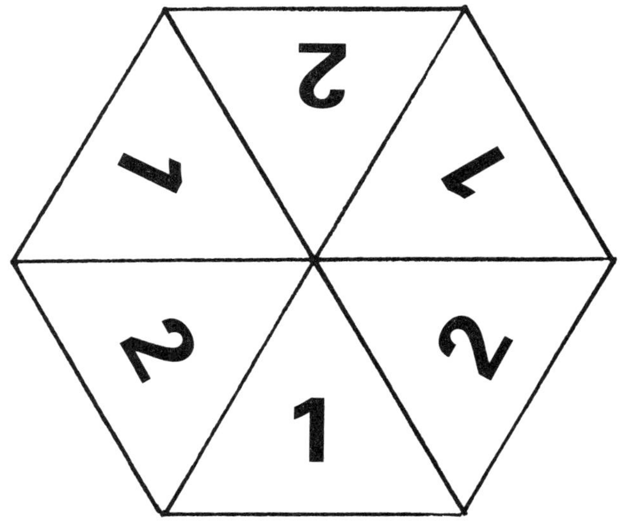

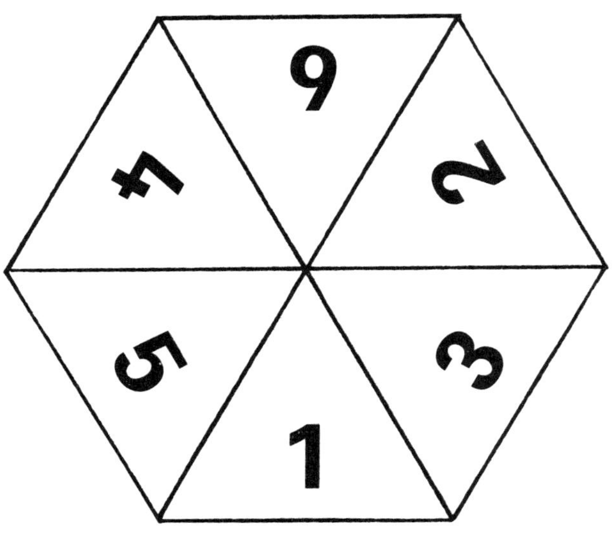

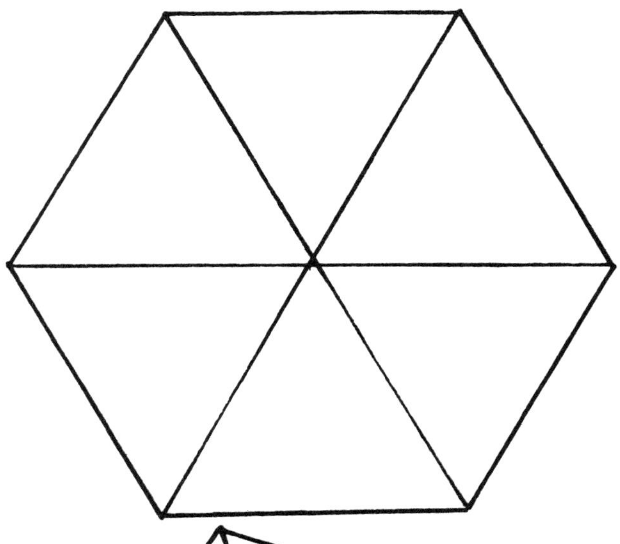

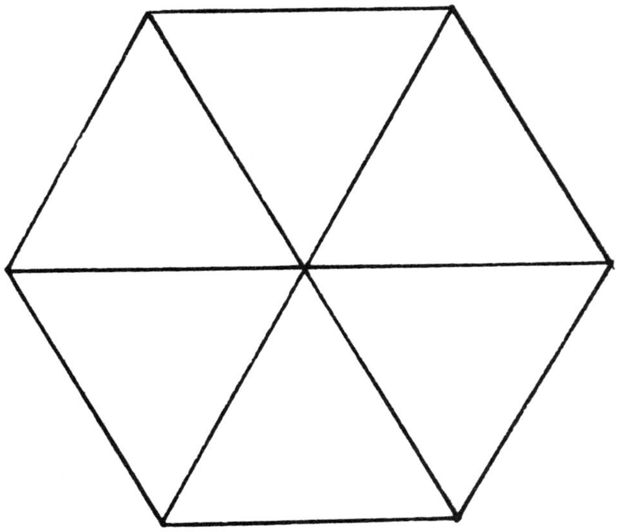

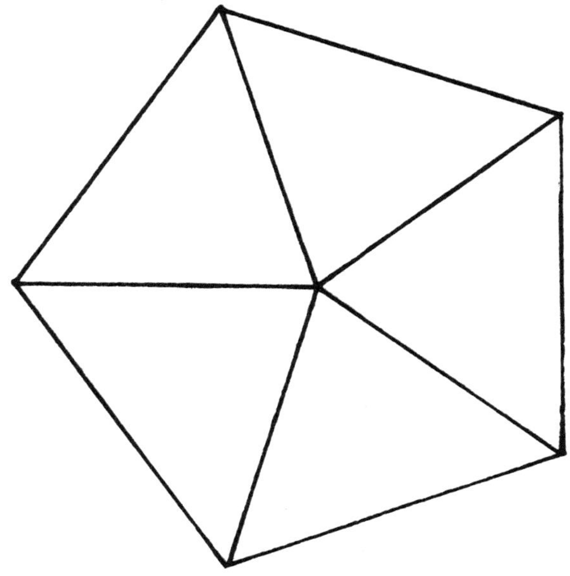

Name ______________________________

Hundred squares

1	2	3	4	5	6	7	8	9	10
11	12	13	14	15	16	17	18	19	20
21	22	23	24	25	26	27	28	29	30
31	32	33	34	35	36	37	38	39	40
41	42	43	44	45	46	47	48	49	50
51	52	53	54	55	56	57	58	59	60
61	62	63	64	65	66	67	68	69	70
71	72	73	74	75	76	77	78	79	80
81	82	83	84	85	86	87	88	89	90
91	92	93	94	95	96	97	98	99	100

Name ______________________________

Large hundred square

1	2	3	4	5	6	7	8	9	10
11	12	13	14	15	16	17	18	19	20
21	22	23	24	2	[illegible]	[illegible]	[illegible]	[illegible]	30
31	32	33	34	3	[illegible]	[illegible]	[illegible]	[illegible]	40
41	42	43	44	4	[illegible]	[illegible]	[illegible]	[illegible]	50
51	52	53	54	5	[illegible]	[illegible]	[illegible]	[illegible]	60
61	62	63	64	65	66	67	68	69	70
71	72	73	74	75	76	77	78	79	80
81	82	83	84	85	86	87	88	89	90
91	92	93	94	95	96	97	98	99	100

Name ______________________

Large squares

Name ______________________

Resource copymaster

Small squares

Name ______________________

Resource copymaster

Dotty squares

Name ______________________________

Dotty triangles

Name ____________________

Resource copymaster

Venn diagram: two discrete sets

Name ____________________

Venn diagram: four discrete sets

Name ______________________________

Resource copymaster

Venn diagram: two overlapping sets

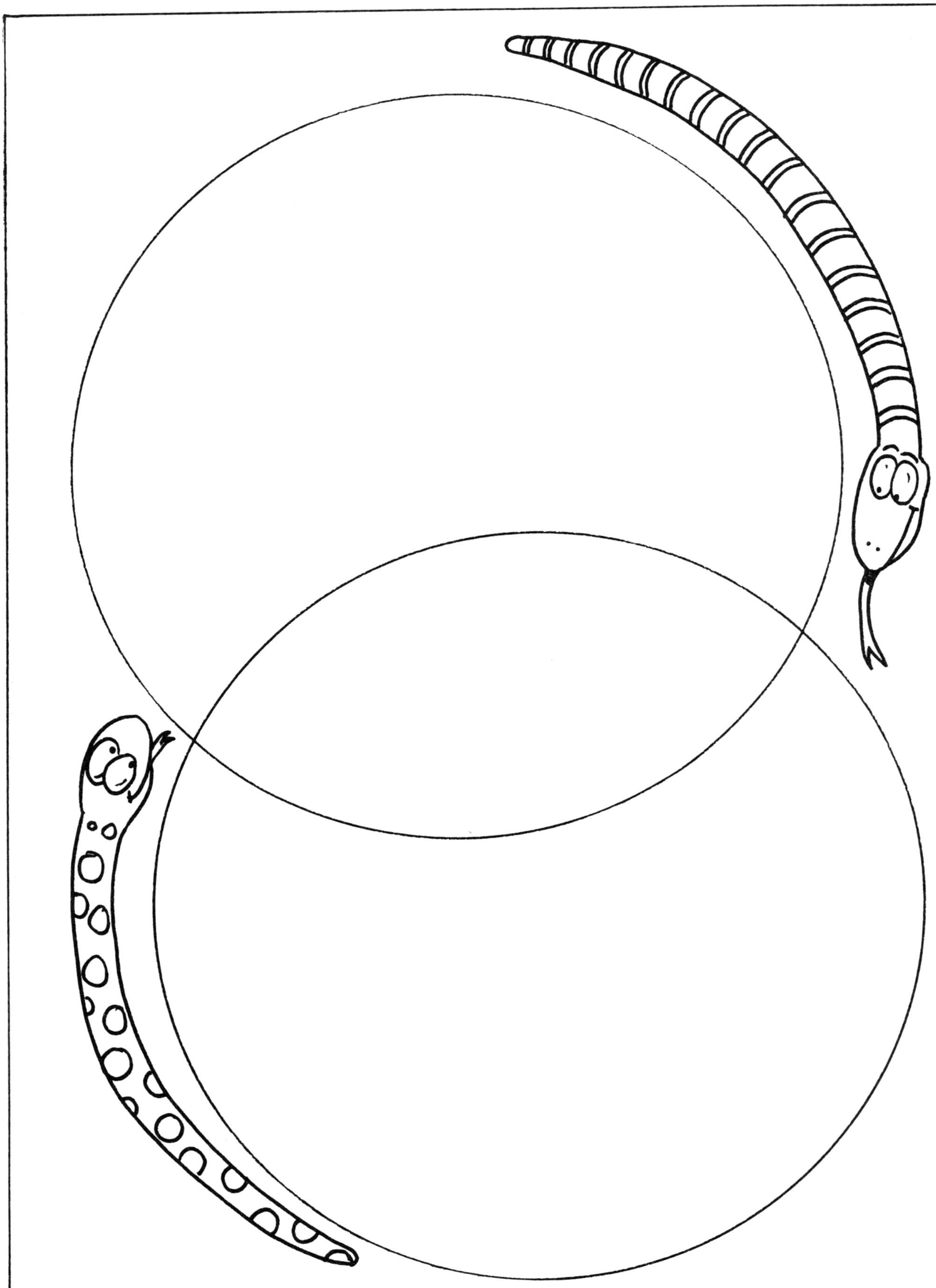

Name ______________________________

Carroll diagram

Record Sheet

Pupil's name ______________________

AT2 Number	1	2	3	4
	5	6	7	8
	9	10	11	12
	13	14	15	16
	17	18	19	20
	21	22	23	24
	25	26	27	28
	29	30	31	32
	33	34	35	36
	37	38	39	40
	41	42	43	44
	45	46	47	48
	49	50	51	52
	53	54	55	56
	57	58	59	60
	61	62	63	64
	65	66	67	68
	69			
AT3 Shape, Space and Measures	70	71	72	73
	74	75	76	77
	78	79	80	81
	82	83	84	85
	86	87	88	89
	90	91	92	93
	94	95	96	97
	98	99	100	101